PERCY

A STORY OF 1918

PERCY

A STORY OF 1918

BY

Peter Doyle

ILLUSTRATIONS
BY

Tim Godden

UNIFORM

UNIFORM

First published by Uniform
an imprint of Unicorn Publishing Group LLP, 2018
5 Newburgh Street
London W1F 7RG
www.unicornpublishing.org

A CIP catalogue record for this book
is available from the British Library.

Text © Peter Doyle
Illustrations © Tim Godden

10 9 8 7 6 5 4 3 2 1

ISBN 978-1-911604-81-5

Design by susanacardona.es

Printed in Spain

One day, a small bundle of letters was found
in a flea market.

Kept together for one hundred years, these few letters
tell of one teenage boy, Percy, and his girl, Kitty.

This is a story of 1918,
and of young people caught up in war,
and of the war itself.

It is a true story.

———

PIT BOY

P ERCY LIVED IN A SMALL MINING VILLAGE in North Wales. He was
a young lad with a fresh complexion, quick blue eyes darting out
from under a huge cap. Slightly built, he was bulked out in rough
tweed, in a jacket that had already seen years of hard use. Yes, Percy
was ready for the pit, his scarf tightly bound around his neck and
tucked into his waistcoat, his legs clad in shabby trousers for warmth.
But it was his boots that truly bore the scars of his calling, of his days
in the mines of Wales, through the pit grime that had been ground
into the very grain of the leather.

The village of his birth was worn, too. No beauty, its streets were
at least built from sturdy materials born of Wales. Red bricks fired
from the clays of Ruabon, roofs clad with slate from Ffestiniog and
Llanberis – the best in the world. And Percy's village sat on stone that
was sought after for the making of grand buildings in the great city of
Liverpool some fifty miles away. This grey-brown stone formed a high
ridge, *cefn mawr* in Welsh, which led to the name of the village that
grew at its very top, a village with a majestic view of the River Dee that
flowed in lazy curves below.

Though the Dee valley was lush and green, the grey village of Cefn had been born of the hungry desires of industrial men who sought to claim the riches below ground. Beneath the rough stone cap of the ridge, there were thick seams of coal and iron – even clay for bricks. It was true that where such minerals were found, there came the chance for the rich to get richer. And to achieve their wealth it required strong men to work the stones, to hew the good coal and iron from the unforgiving embrace of worthless rock.

'JACK!' cried Percy as he stood in the gloom outside his friend's little house.

'Jack! We'll be late!' A sleepy head appeared at the window and nodded, blear-eyed. Percy had done his duty by his friend. Neither of them could afford to be late to the pit. Wrapped up against the cold, as usual with cap pulled down and muffler tucked into his waistcoat, Percy went back to his own cottage to collect his things.

Percy's cottage sat with six other simple houses in what had once been a quarry, a hole cut into the very top of Cefn's ridge. Even today the history of Cefn is written in the streets that seem to emerge from the ridge: Rock Hill, Rock Lane, Rock Place sit near to the more hopeful Mount Pleasant. While some of these nestled close to

nature, Percy's row of houses was not pretty, and the red bricks of the cottages jarred against the jumble of blocks and the teetering rock faces of the old quarry.

For all its untidiness, the quarry was a good place for lads to grow up, offering up many adventures. It was here that Percy and Jack had fought the play-wars of childhood, games of hide-and-seek and rough-and-tumble amongst the unforgiving rocks, and had comforted each other as they grazed their shins and banged their heads.

'Yes, they were grand times,' Percy muttered under his breath and thrust his hands deeper into his pockets as he saw the glowering shapes of the quarry appear out of the gloom. But right now, Percy needed to make sure he and Jack could get to the pit on time.

'HI, Percy, wait!' Jack joined his friend and they swung purposefully down the road, their snap-tins and billy-cans banging against their legs as they headed down the slope towards their coal pit. Both trod a path that had been well worn by countless miners before them.

While the pit cottages of Cefn, tied to the coalmines of Ruabon, were graceless, the landscape around them was breath-taking. The valley of the Dee stretched away to the town of Llangollen, and was occupied by man-made routes, of railways and canals that transported the riches of Wales to the industrial cities of England.

As his strong pit boots scraped loudly against the paved streets, Percy's thoughts were with his girl, Kitty, a servant in the grand hall on the other side of the Dee.

'Do you think Gertie would have time to walk out this Sunday?' said Percy to Jack. Gertie was Jack's sweetheart, and the four of them were as thick as thieves, strolling out along the fast flowing river, skimming stones and watching the dippers darting around the shallows, the birds picking out insects and other juicy morsels.

Percy had always felt responsible for the younger lad, his best pal, above and below ground. When all four of them, Percy and Kitty, Jack and Gertie, walked arm-in-arm along the streets of Llangollen in the summer-days, or later sat in tea-shops by the fast-flowing Dee, they were a sight. Passers-by could not help but smile at the joy of them.

Yes, Percy was blessed with the most glorious countryside that had once framed his childish games and pranks, but which now served as a backdrop to the love he felt for his friends. But there was no time for the two lads to get sentimental. They had men's work to do.

Childhood had been short for Percy. Like Jack and many of his friends, Percy had been a pit boy from the age of fourteen. It had always been so. Generations of boys before them had worked in the coalmines from an even younger age. With no chance of education, and coming from very poor families, the young pit boys of earlier times had helped their fathers and mothers to bring home some coppers, coins like farthings and ha'pennies, to put some food on the table – but could neither read, nor write. Then, there were no laws to keep them in school.

But for Percy and his best pal, things were different in Edwardian Britain. Unlike past ages, now the Government made sure that both lads had stayed at school until they were thirteen, busy with their reading, writing and arithmetic – and it was not always appreciated.

As Percy and Jack had sat together in the cold school room, they stared out of the window at the men walking down the valley to the mine works, chemical factories and brick kilns with their tall chimneys spewing smoke.

'It'll be us next, Percy', whispered Jack, as the stern-faced teacher bent to her blackboard and scraped the chalk over its well-used surface.

For the moment though, Percy had to half concentrate on his lessons. Only half concentrate, mind, because while his family spoke the lyrical language of his ancestors, he was being taught only to read and write in English, the language of the Empire. At school, he learned how best to write a letter from his class books and teachers with chalk-dusted fingers.

'It gives me great pleasure to answer your ever welcome letter' he would start, quickly running out of steam, yet finishing with the small regret 'I have no more to say this time so I will close.' His letters would never change. Not even in war.

English language in the classroom; but no English laws would stop Welsh being spoken at home or below ground, and every night the joy of the ancient language resonated around his cottage as the oil-lamps flickered. Late into evening, with a eye still yet on the clock, the two boys' fathers talked over the business of the Ruabon mines, sharing glasses of beer as dark as the very coal they cut from the hills with the sweat of their labour, cheers! *Lechyd da*!

Pit boys. Percy and Jack. Mates arm-in-arm. They seemed invincible in the valley of the Dee, but were not so below ground. Here coal hewers hacked the blackest of fuel-rocks from beneath the crushing weight of the Welsh hills, while about them the pit boys weaved in and out of the dark, dark, tunnels grime-faced. In awe of the face miners, the boys opened trap doors, looked after the pit ponies, helped fill mine trucks; they did whatever they were told, and went wherever they could to be helpful, and to catch an extra copper coin from the top men. One day, perhaps one day, they would earn the right to be king of the miners, the hewer. But until that day they stuck to their work.

Percy's *tada* was a hewer. He'd been granted that position through hard labour, as *his* own father had before him. Tough and wiry, Benjamin had learned what it was like to drive his pick into the brittle, splintery, black coal. Yet, though hard, it was not work for big men. A big, wide-shouldered man would have become hopelessly stuck. Percy's father would more often than not have to squeeze himself between unforgiving rock seams to hack at the coal that reflected the dim flame of his safety lamp. And when this was won, he would drive back the face with hammers and wedges so that he could once more get to the precious coal. Working for eight-hour shifts, for six days a week, his muscles became iron-hard, his skin toughened by the black, black dust.

There was no greater hero for Percy than his *tada*.

In 1918, at fifty-three years of age, Benjamin was the proud father of seven healthy children – though he had buried three others, who had died tragically, so young. His oldest son Thomas, now twenty-nine years of age, had also reached the goal of being a hewer. Like Percy, he'd worked his way up, sticking close to his father, filling coal trucks in the gloom.

Now respected at the coal face, Thomas regularly batted his younger brother's ears as he went by in the dim light of the mine galleries; no other boys would dare cross Percy though – for they knew they would have the young hewer to deal with. (Jack also knew that, and kept close to his friend in the black voids). In the tight-knit community of Cefn Mawr, the pride of the Edwards family was clear to see.

There were other working voices in that tiny, brick-built cottage too. There was David, and the younger Benjamin. Neither had taken the path of the hewer, choosing instead to toil in the brick-yards of Ruabon. Quietly, their father was glad. The black heart of the coalmines had claimed too many lives since they had opened. Yet for David and the young Benjamin, their destiny was not grounded in the clay of Ruabon, but in the mud of Flanders – to become part of the British Army. For in 1914 the country needed more coal than bricks, and even more – it needed soldiers.

Percy had taken his place as pit boy in the mines at fourteen in 1914. War loomed on the horizon, but he paid it little heed, as all he had dreamt of was being a hewer – not a soldier. To him, his calling to the mines seemed inevitable, just as son followed father. And it was expected.

Even then Percy was not the youngest lad in the house; there was also Caradoc. Still at the school, while the others toiled in the depths, the youngest boy worked at his slate with his rough stylus, and bent over the rough wooden desk, so covered in ink patches as black as coal dust. (He too would face life in the pit, when his time would come.)

While Percy and Caradoc busied themselves in the life of the village, they barely noticed that conflict had arrived on Britain's doorstep. But it was hard to miss the change in the clanking of the pit gear and the smoke of the chemical factories; there was a greater urgency as the nation geared for war.

By 1918, there was no avoiding the war. The hard battle-years of 1915, 1916 and 1917 had cost the lives of many Welsh boys, names listed in forlorn ranks in the daily papers. Now there was a growing threat to the Allies in France, a threat that meant that the army's need for men was the greatest it had ever been.

In 1918, one thing was certain. Pit boys were not hewers. But they could be soldiers. And their time in the army of the King would come, as night follows day.

CYMRU

A SMALL COUNTRY, THE LAND OF WALES is rugged and enticing, shaped by titanic forces back in the depths of Earth's history that created the jagged, dark peaks of the north, and the desolate uplands of the south. In both, rich earth disguised even greater riches below ground, with minerals that would help build the industry of Britain. From these landscapes and the towns and remote villages came men and women who were used to hardship. And they were to sacrifice much in the war of four years.

Cymru, that beautiful land, bore also deep scars inflicted on nature by man. For people came in search of metals for their tools, stone for their houses, and coal for their fuel. Quarries were sunk ever deeper into the land of Wales to seek out the best materials. Here, Welsh slate was wrenched from these open scars to be sent across the world – leaving mountains in their wake as wreckages of waste. And while these wounds were inflicted, families toiled beneath the surface to hew the brittle-black substance that nature had bestowed upon Wales.

Old Ben's pick sank deeply into the blackest of coal seams. Stripped to the waste, he was grimed by the dust that seemed to fill

every pore. His breathing was deep; the air was thin, and with each strike, the dust swirled around him. As he lay labouring on his side beneath the weight of the coal, his mind was blank, his arms working to deliver the unrelenting strike of the pick. Over, and over, and over.

'I think *tada* is at the face by here' shouted Percy over the sound of the coal tubs clanking by. He and Jack were making sure they were full, so the face men like his father got their full rate.

'I hope he's safe'

'*Duw*, bach, your da will live forever!' shouted Jack over the din, picking up a mighty lump of coal and throwing it into the truck.

But Percy knew the coughing was getting worse.

British industry had been built by King Coal. It was the coal resources found deep underground that had fuelled the Industrial Revolution, and it was coal that helped forge the iron and steel that birthed the machines of war. These weapons became ever more complex as the conflict rolled on, the science of killing becoming even more despicable. There were bigger guns, bigger shells, bigger ships, tanks even: there seemed no end to the list. And while there was no end to war's insatiable appetite, the industry to make these relied upon men and women, the raw materials and, above all, coal.

Coal and more coal.

In the deep valleys of Wales there were mines – pits – that were already a century old. As the war came in 1914 there were over two-hundred-and-thirty thousand men working below ground in South Wales alone, producing almost sixty million tons of coal. With Britain was ever more hungry for this fuel, the men emerging from these pits came forth filthy with the black earth they had hewn from the deepest depths.

Their toil was hard, and when tragedy struck – with roof collapses and explosions – the effects were felt deeply throughout the close-knit communities. And even though the newspapers had carried the news since 1914 of Welshmen who died in war, it was still a shock to hear when a miner had been killed below ground in pursuit of coal – especially if that miner was a pit boy.

It was Percy's way to look through the paper with his mam on a Saturday. Still grimed from the pit he'd pick up a copy as he wound his way up the steep High Street to good old Rock Place. There was news of the town and the Chapel, notices and events; but one such day, suddenly, Percy was pulled up from his reading. It was as if a cold hand had gripped him.

'Cefn lad killed in an Astley Pit', read the headline.

'We feel sure that our readers will join us in expressing deep sympathy with Mr and Mrs Valentine of Stevens Terrace, Cefn, on the death of their eldest son, Thom…'

Percy broke off from his reading. Thomas Owen Valentine was a pal from school, a mate to Jack and him. And he'd been crushed by the mine trucks in a far away pit in Lancashire.

Percy folded the paper confused about the death. Tom was his age, a pit boy just like him. He closed his eyes and tried to be strong. With

Jack, he'd seen many close calls with those trucks. But for a young lad like Tom to be killed…

He was quiet that evening, alone with his thoughts. He would still face the walk to the pit the next day, nevertheless. And he would call upon Jack, just as he always did.

The Welsh were no strangers to tragedy. And surely, they would see more, yet.

For South Wales at least, where coal was abundant, there was an even bigger prize – steam coal – the 'food of the engines' of the battleships of the British Grand Fleet. Steam coal produced much energy when eaten up by ships' boilers, and, best of all, it gave off little smoke to attract enemies at sea. It was the secret weapon of the British Navy, and Wales was its supplier. Without steam coal, and the hard graft of men and women of Wales, most ships would be nothing more than iron hulks, and Britain would be in grave danger.

In South Wales, whole communities of mining villages grew up in the valleys that would become justly famous. They were not the most picturesque of places. Built to serve the ever-more hungry desire for coal, they were described as 'long dreary rows of drab houses with filthy and haphazard streets'. These streets were further oppressed with an atmosphere of smoke and coal dust, and were unhealthy to live in.

Less well known, though, were the mining villages that grew up in the shadow of the mountains of Snowdonia; one of them, Percy's home. By a quirk of geography, North Wales has a coalfield that is found beneath the surface near Wrexham, Ruabon and eastwards towards England. In this small part of a small country, there were many small mines, as adventurers and investors attempted to cash in on the need for black gold wrenched from the very Earth.

And while the South Wales coal was needed for ships, North Wales coal was needed as a fuel at home, dug from sixty mines scattered around Wrexham. It was the coal of North Wales that burned brightly and gave off more heat than that from the south – perfect for Britain's damp, cold climate.

Mrs Edwards reached over to the scuttle and picked out some likely chunks of the blackest coal, blocks that reflected the glow of the embers in the grate. She never failed in making the lives of those in the cottage warm and bright. And it was the coal that her husband had dug that linked them together in that warmth. Not only that; it was the very fuel of the home fires that were sung about in 1914, words from a hit song from a Welsh boy that carried meaning for every family in war.

Keep the Home Fires Burning,
While your hearts are yearning.
Though your lads are far away
They dream of home.

'They dream of home'. The link the song made between its home fires and its soldier boys was surely no stronger than in North Wales.

And from its mines Percy emerged, also of this land, to eventually take his part in the war. He too would dream of home, when the time came.

FOR KING AND COUNTRY

'WALES MUST DO HER DUTY. I should like to see a Welsh Army in the field. I should like to see the race that faced the Norman for hundreds of years in a struggle for freedom give a good taste of its quality in this struggle in Europe; AND THEY ARE GOING TO DO IT!'

David Lloyd George, the Chancellor of the Exchequer, stood down from the podium exhausted. He had given the speech of his life in the capital of the Empire. War was not what he had wanted, no; but there had been no choice. The little nation of Belgium had been invaded, and the fight had become inevitable. And now it was up to him to help build a new army to win that fight.

Lloyd George was a proud Welshman, equal in his lyrical language to the great poets and songsters that had made his nation famous. And with his speech, the Welsh Chancellor had shaken the whole country out of a deep sleep, and awoken it to the reality of war. And though the Welsh were naturally at home with peace, their minister had persuaded them that there was an urgent need to rise up and fight the tyrants of war, and that small nations should not be ignored.

So it was that Wales became involved in conflict on a gloriously warm summer's bank holiday in August 1914. Bands played cheerily on the seaside promenade at the wonderful Welsh resort of Llandudno, the seagulls wheeling over the elegant bay, the sun and a sea breeze playing on the backs of the couples that strolled along the handsome pier. The storm clouds were gathering on the continent of Europe, but even then, the threat of war seemed too remote to dampen the holiday mood, and to spoil the many picnics that had spread out on rough rugs across the yellow sands.

Walking along the elegant promenade, with the sun beating down on parasols and boaters, there was no need to worry. After all, if war came, it would be short, and fought far away from the distant shores of England, yes? Britain's mighty navy, pride of the nation, and its highly trained army would surely see to that?

Such weighty questions seemed so very remote from the streets of a pit village, tucked away in the hills of North Wales.

At home in Cefn Mawr, Percy's mam busied herself in the small kitchen, cooking bakestones on her iron griddle. Beside his mother was her teenage son, scanning the front pages of the newspapers that were spread out on the rough kitchen table, with the even younger children playing marbles at its feet.

Percy was looking for news from Europe; he saw instead, as he had always done, the local merchants like Mr Richards, or Mr Jones of Well Street, advertising their wares, and news of tempting day trips. There was no mention of a crisis. No, it was business as usual in peaceful Wales, and Percy was content.

War was at their doorstep, but coal miner Benjamin had seen it all before. He knew how quickly these things got out of hand, and his first thoughts were with his boys. All too well could he remember 1899, when conflict had broken out in far-away South Africa. Then it was rough Dutch-speaking Boer farmers rebelling against British rule.

Now the enemy was to be a whole nation, and a most powerful one at that; truly there was no value in war.

'*Tad*!' *Tada*! The *Chronicle* says there's to be a war!' Percy was barely fourteen, and the prospect of war seemed enticing.

'Put that by, boy,' said his father in a low voice. Benjamin knew that the Boer War had started this way. Full of excitement, ideas of heroic charges and of valiant deeds. He would have none of that. Too many good men still lay in the Transvaal. And Benjamin had five sons.

'Put away any thoughts of far-away wars, son. You've got work to do at the pit', he growled, 'They'll be needing you there'.

But Percy still thought of the deeds of Empire he'd seen in the pictures.

Lloyd George's words of 1914 had been published, and so it was that every detail of the speech was pored over, across the land of his forefathers. And in the dimly-lit miner's cottage on the rough stone cap of Cefn, Percy stared at the words, barely comprehending what they could mean to his family.

But for David and Benjamin, the Welsh minister's words carried power, his sentences posing a challenge.

Yes, their minds were made up. They would enlist. After all, the older boys had seen the posters; notices calling men to the army that had begun to appear in the windows of every Post Office, and which popped up in the pages of every newspaper.

YOUR KING AND COUNTRY NEED YOU.
MOBILISATION
GOD SAVE THE KING!

'Come, Dai *bach*' said Ben in a barely concealed whisper, 'Come, before the recruiting office closes. We can catch it if we're quick!'

Quietly they left the cottage and shut the door behind them.

Benjamin and David volunteered to serve in Royal Welsh Fusiliers, the historic regiment of North Wales; soldiers who were no strangers to battle, but who, in turn, would become known as poets – in the aftermath of war.

The new men of the Royal Welsh would be gathered into a great division, a body of thousands, all marked by the Red Dragon of Wales. And Ben and Dai Edwards were to become one with them.

In truth, it was a shock for Percy when two of his older brothers 'answered the call'. But David and Benjamin had tired of the clay pits. With his eldest brother, Thomas, needed in the mines, the two other Edwards boys had purposefully pulled on their heavy jackets to make their way to the recruiting office in Llangollen. Duty had to be done, and digging clay could wait; they would follow the words of Lloyd George. But little did Dai and Ben know that they would be destined to dig the heavy soil of Flanders, as they had once dug the clay of Ruabon.

Percy remembered the two oldest boys coming back to the cottage, while their family waited. He remembered them pushing open the door with a determined shove, and the desperate gasp his mother let out as she saw the light blue enlistment papers grasped tightly in their hands.

'Don't take on so, mam!' snorted David, as he drew his simple chair abruptly over the rough flagstone floor and sat down in a determined manner.

'The war will be over by Christmas, and we'll be wanting to do our bit, so we will!'

Dai tossed his King's Shilling on the table, his first day's wages in the British Army. The coin span, and came ominously and finally to rest on the hard surface. For the briefest of moments there was silence.

The war would not be over by Christmas. No, and the boys would not be coming back, not yet. In fact, Britain would need many, many more boys before the war was done.

THE GREAT WAR

A S 1914 DREW TO A CLOSE, if it had been possible to look down on the continent of Europe from on high, then two lines of ditches would be seen, facing each other for 350 miles from the Swiss border to the shore of the North Sea. These ditches had soon become filled with men, who daily struggled to overcome the odds in a brutal fight for survival. This was trench warfare.

For sure, the trenches had stopped the war in its tracks back in 1914, but soon these hateful ditches had become oh-so-hard for the soldiers to escape. For four long years men peered into the gloom across no-man's-land to the Germans beyond, fearful of what might become of them. Though at times there were battles and smaller, brutal attacks called trench raids, mostly it was the job of a soldier to simply keep himself safe over those four long years of war. And this job was hard. Oh so hard.

It was early in 1915 before the older Edwards boys finally took their places in the ranks of the Royal Welsh Fusiliers, one of the noblest regiments of all. Even then there was much training to be done to get them ready for war. It was a long time yet before they would see for themselves the reality of 'the trenches' – as the newspapers liked to call the frontline.

Before then, to build them up, and to make soldiers from quarrymen, David and Benjamin were destined to train in Wales and England for a year until their legs ached of marching and their arms tired of their rifles. Moving from camp to camp they saw more of Britain than they had ever done before. And when they had finally arrived on the great plain of Salisbury, they saw that it was marked with vast encampments of tents which spread across the landscape, seeming almost to merge with the horizon.

Then, as 1915 drew to a close, their training in England at an end, the Edwards boys had crossed the sea from England to France, feeling the breeze on their faces, just as they had done on the rough boards of the pier at Llandudno in times of peace. Though now it was war, and there was still a lot of war to be done. The relentless throb of the troopship engines beneath their feet carried them ever closer to conflict.

When the Welshmen of the Red Dragon – the boys of the Royal Welsh – arrived in France they were once more thrust onto the training field. But now it was different; their instructors had a desperate urgency in their voices, a hardness born of battle experiences that made them force their men to charge up the sandhills of the French coast, and to carry out bayonet drills accompanied by terrifying screams.

'These boys need to be ready', thought the Sergeant instructor as he bawled out his orders, his chest marked by medal ribbons of past wars; he knew all too well of the terrible hardships his boys would have to face.

Through it all, David and Benjamin thought often of the craggy hilltop at Cefn, and of the clay pits of Ruabon.

And before they knew, the time of training had passed. Then the Edwards boys climbed silently onto one of the drab, boarded and battered omnibuses that lined the road dolefully. These once homely vehicles had been torn from the streets of London to be sent to 'the front' – just like the soldiers who clambered aboard them, their world changed forever.

Up the line, and at the front, the brothers had to endure great hardships, but could say little in their few postcards home, written in snatched moments between duty. Their letters from the front were equally sparse. In between pleasantries, the Edwards boys spoke ominously of their journey 'up the line', and hinted at the challenges they faced, eking out their daily lives 'in the trenches'.

Percy stared with wonder at the cards his brothers had sent, as they spilled through the letterbox onto the hard floor of the cottage. They depicted ruined streets in France and Belgium, and it was difficult to make out the names of the villages, which had been so crudely scratched out. This was so as not to give the game away to the Germans – if the mail was somehow to fall into enemy hands. Uncomprehending, Percy turned the thin cards over in his hands.

'Hope this finds you in the pink as it leaves me' said Dai one day to his mother in a postcard sent at the end of 1915.

Fifteen-year-old Percy too, read this and wondered. Would he too feel 'in the pink', meaning fit and well, if he was 'Somewhere in France'?

'I am going in the trenches tomorrow', wrote Ben.

('That ruined village on the front of the card could almost have been Cefn, if ever the war came to Wales', Percy thought to himself.)

As the Edwards brothers moved into the trenches at the Somme the old hands cried out 'Keep yer napper down, mate', the cheery cry of old soldiers to the new ones.

But, still, the unwary chanced a peep over the parapet, and many paid the price for it. There were bullets fired into the dark, and shells shot from guns far away. Hoping that, by poor luck and terrible chance, these weapons would not seek out a mate was all that soldiers could do; and to try and protect them, many carried charms and treasures from home. In truth, they didn't often work.

Instead, the Edwards boys stuck to their duty, and learned the trade of the soldier – though they thought of Cefn, often. (Their copy-ink pencil postcards could say little about what they really thought.)

'We've had a bit of fine weather, please send some Keating's powder if you can', wrote David one fine spring morning, as the shells whistled above his head. It was normal. Usual. Just the way things were 'in the trenches'.

'MAM!' What's Keating's powder for? shouted Percy, as he scanned the card for hidden details, yet not finding them.

'Never mind, boy!', said his mother sharply, knowing full well that it was to kill body lice. She shivered slightly with the horror of it.

Nevertheless, she vowed to pop down to Mr Jones at the Pharmacy. After all, he advertised 'I.K. Insect Killer. Kills fleas, Body Lice, etc. Send one in your next parcel to the front.' Disgusting insects; no boy of hers would have to suffer lice if *she* could help it. No, she'd talk to Mr Jones to make that right.

Often, there were other soldiers' letters to read, letters published in the newspapers, in the good old *Cefn Chronicle*. It seemed that there was a tender link between the soldiers across the sea and their little home in the green land of Wales. Mr and Mrs Edwards looked out for names they knew, trying to fill in the spaces between their sons' brief cards with the tales told by the sons of other families from the village. And between their many stories of heroic deeds, there were others that told of daily life, of dugouts, shells and bully beef, of real tales of survival, and of the truth of the trenches.

'The rats are so numerous that it is impossible to sleep long' wrote Corporal Lowell of the good old RWF, 'for they run all over us, so you can guess how I feel…' Once again, Mrs Edwards shuddered inwardly while she sipped her tea and scanned the paper.

There were other parents in the village who endured, and who regularly scoured the pages of the *Chronicle* for news. There was old Mr Hughes of Rock Terrace, a street off Cefn's rocky top, just doors away from the Edwards' cosy mining cottage. His son John did not have to go; after all, he was 35 and a hewer. He'd joined anyway. But it was not long before Lance Corporal Hughes of the RWF was in the thick of the action, regularly writing home in 1916, months before the great battle on the Somme.

'We were ordered to make a raid on the German trenches', Corporal Hughes explained. 'We crept over the 250 yards of ground and lay by the barbed wire, when we received the order to rush the trench'. His letter to the *Chronicle* was stirring stuff, and Mr Edwards examined his neighbour's words intently by the light of an old oil lamp. Were his boys at this very moment lying out in front of the enemy trenches, in the black of a Somme night?

For the boys in the trenches, as summer turned to winter, the solid walls the men had spent their nights repairing became crumbling earth or rain-sodden mud. Sleep was scarce and food poor. The fatigue was numbing. Soldiers learned to live with lice, rats and, in the summer, hoards of flies.

Gradually, people at home got used to the idea that the war was one of 'sticking it out' in damp ditches, facing the enemy. It became accepted that the life in these trenches was one of long periods of boredom interrupted by short periods of terror. And the whole time, the families waited for their soldiers to return; hoping, always hoping.

At home, their minds full of pictures from the patriotic magazines, everyone thought of the 'poor blighters' in the trenches, and did their best to send letters, comforts and parcels. With care, Mrs Edwards packed up boxes for her boys in the trenches. Keatings, yes; but also sweets, candles, writing paper, socks, anything to help David and Benjamin get by.

Percy and Jack would be sent down into the village to buy such comforts from Mr Richards' general store with the few coppers they could pull together. And in these parcels Percy sent notes that expressed his love for his older brothers.

For deep inside the pit boy knew that, one day, it would be *he* who would wait for parcels from home while shivering in the trenches.

SERVANT GIRL

Mining was not the only industry in North Wales.

In the mid-nineteenth century, Robert Graesser came from Saxony to settle in the valley of the Dee. He had his eye on the Welsh mines, and planned to bring his industrial know-how from Germany to create a chemical factory. In Ruabon, Graesser transformed a by-product of the mining industry – coal tar – into an antiseptic called carbolic acid, and grew rich on the back of it. And when, eventually, war came, Graesser's chemical factory would make the explosives for shells that would be fired at his countrymen – it was perhaps as well that old Mr Graesser himself would not live to see this happen.

While the industry sprawled in Ruabon, Robert Graesser's fortune mounted, and so did his growing family. Together they moved to the slopes of the Dee Valley, to the village of Vron (its name taken from the Welsh for slope, *fron*), facing Cefn's ridge. Here, in Argoed Hall, the Graesser family enjoyed the clean air, beautiful views and landscaped gardens, and lived very different lives indeed from the pit, iron and chemical workers of Cefn Mawr.

Argoed Hall was indeed a grand house. It had already stood for a century when Mr Graesser bought it, and it was built of the best bricks that Ruabon could supply. Orange and terracotta, it was a jewel set in a woodland that tumbled down the valley slopes to the Dee, and had both kennels and stables for the Graessers' enjoyment, as well as a coach house for their convenience. In this idyllic setting, Robert and his wife Mary brought up a strapping family. Each of their four sons would follow their father's path into chemistry – and none would have to soldier, to fight against their father's homeland, when the world turned to war in 1914. After all, trained scientists were in short supply in wartime Britain.

The Graessers were not the only people to live at the Hall. Then, wealthy families living upstairs in big halls could afford to pay for servants, people who would live downstairs and out of sight of the family and their grand guests. This was the case at Argoed. Here was the lady's maid to look after the needs of Mrs Graesser. Then there was the cook, called upon to serve up Saxon delicacies such as *Sauerbraten* or *Biergulasch*, or just simply home-grown Welsh lamb. And then there were the 'General Domestic' servants, usually young women, whose job it was to keep their grand families comfortable and well fed. And so it was that at the outbreak of war, in 1914, England and Wales could boast that it had more servants at home than men in the army.

There was no doubt that Cook was in charge below stairs.

'Kitty! KITTY! Get along girl!' Cook was a kindly person, but when the Graesser's were entertaining their guests there was no time for gossiping.

'Find me that large roasting tin!' There was pork that needed a good roast, and though her employers were good people, they liked everything *alles richtig*!

Kitty was just sixteen. Her father was a butcher's delivery-man from London – the family lived in Chelsea on the King's Road. This is a very posh place now, but not so a hundred years ago. Then and now, though, the street would be full of shoppers and people intent on their daily lives. And Kitty's father would go on his rounds delivering his meat to his customers, meat freshly butchered and gathered from London's historic Smithfield Market. His day started early in the morning, at five o'clock – essential if he was to get on his rounds and keep his regulars happy.

Kitty was a bright girl with a London accent, her unruly hair tucked under her hat, her complexion fresh but her hands tinged with a redness that spoke of a willingness to work hard; she would need that. But in truth, people meeting her and her mother together on the streets of London would notice something different about the family, a distinction between the two.

Dewch draw Kitty, *mae 'siopa i'w wneud!*, said her mother, as Kitty dawdled in front of the shop fronts. There was shopping to be done!

For Kitty's mother was a native Welsh speaker, born of the lush green hills of North Wales.

Just like Kitty would later become, her mother Susan before her had been a servant from a young age. Working in the Butcher's Arms pub, no doubt she was attracted by the cheerful and talkative London butcher who just happened to wander into her Welsh inn one fateful day. She was destined to marry her Londoner and follow him to 'the Smoke', as the capital of the British Empire was nick-named, a result of the great number of chimneys that burned Welsh coal, and of the acrid smoke that clogged the air and blackened the bricks. How could this hope to compare with Wales? Susan would hope that one day her family would see the land of her fathers.

Argoed Hall was in need of bright girls to keep its rooms spick and span, and like her mother before her, Kitty was taken on to carry out the domestic chores. Leaving the bustling streets of London, she arrived in North Wales, following the dreams of her mother. As one of the youngest in the hall, only very few times would Kitty appear in the bright and gay rooms that rang with the laughter of the Graessers' extended family. Instead, she would work in its depths, in the cellars, on her knees cleaning floors and shooing away noisome insects that lurked in its corners.

'Urgh, disgusting cockroaches' thought Kitty, once more fixing her hair as the bugs scattered with the sound of clicking on the flag floors. She would have to deal with them later.

Kitty was not alone at the hall though. She took comfort that she had her best friend at her side, a General Domestic just like her. Gertie was a sweet Welsh girl, just 15 years of age, with bright eyes sparkling from an innocent face, a face eager to please.

But it was often that Cook would chase the two giggling girls, shouting at them with sharp words to 'clean the pots and be quick about it!'

Secretly, Cook smiled to herself, remembering the carefree start of her own life in the hills of Wales. Times were harder now.

It was always to Sundays that Kitty and Gertie looked, as it was then that they could escape the Hall and see their sweethearts, their pit boys, Percy and Jack.

'Gertie, do you think we will be able to see the boys tonight?' Kitty was ever hopeful, but the life of a General Domestic was a hard one.

'Depends on Cook' said Gertie. She knew that if the meal had gone well, Cook's round face would look kindly on her two girls. *If* the meal had gone well, mind.

And Kitty was always fearful of losing her position. It *was* a long way back to London, after all. She'd been late back on several occasions, and couldn't afford to do it again.

'Well, I hope so', thought Kitty, 'We don't want those boys chasing other girls.'

Kitty's boy was Percy. If there was any doubt, his letters to her made that plain. Sealed in small blue envelopes, the love Percy felt for his servant girl was written on the outside for all to see. At a time when small things meant everything, the way Percy placed his one-penny stamps on the letter was important. Percy's stamps leaned tellingly to the left: in the Edwardian language of stamps, and without him having to utter a real word, this spoke plainly to Kitty: 'I Love You'. (Not that he had said that, of course. He let the *stamps* do the talking.)

'I hope nobody is down in the cellar when you go there on Sunday night,' wrote Percy to Kitty, one day before the war crowded his thoughts. 'When you are going down just think what I said to you the other night.' Just  imagine what he might have said. The cellars were a frighteningly dark place to work. Did he wish her luck, or ask her to think of him?

In truth, their times together were the briefest possible, and the four friends could meet up for fleeting moments only. Kitty and Percy, Gertie and Jack.

'I am glad to hear you are having tomorrow off and I will come and meet you if it is raining or snowing or whatever it is doing,' Percy wrote, in the days before war clouded their view. 'My bicycle touched the ground about twice … I was going over hedges and all,' in his hurry to be with her.

Between the two girls in Vron and the pit boys in Cefn was more than hedges; there was the yawning expanse of the Dee valley, a great natural barrier that separated them. A very great barrier indeed.

But in that valley is also a wonder of the Industrial Revolution. Built by the master engineer Thomas Telford, an immense bridge of nineteen spans crosses the River Dee from slope to slope. Built of Cefn stone and from iron smelted in a nearby foundry, the bridge was a marvel of its age. It was not constructed to carry road traffic – instead it hosted a canal along which narrow boats plied their trade, carrying the fruits of the labour in the quarries, mines and works of Cefn to across the country.

The old bridge was much more than just an engineering marvel; it meant more to the people of Cefn and Vron than that. For it was across the Pontcysyllte Aqueduct that Percy met Kitty, and Kitty met Percy. The quickest route to each other was across the dizzying heights of the great bridge, then a century-old marvel of engineering. Crossing the great valley, Percy relied on the luminous numbers of his prized wristwatch, and on the wheels of his trusty bicycle, to make sure he arrived on time. He was nervous, nonetheless.

'I wish I'd pumped up those tyres', thought Percy as his bike wobbled on the narrow footpath, 'and those brakes need looking at'.

Still, never mind, he would soon be across, and there was no time to stop. Time was precious, and nothing would stand in his way, so long as the Graessers – and cook – could spare their servant girl.

Many a time Kitty would wait at the gate of the Graessers' hall, her brow knitted with worry, Percy late from his work in the pit. There were many dangers.

'Now you must not be disappointed again this week, so keep your pecker up, it will soon be Sunday and if I don't meet with another accident like I did in the Cefn I will come and meet you', wrote Percy to Kitty, one typical day.

Disappointed, yes, but each time he was late, Kitty hoped against hope that he had safely navigated the narrow path, 126 feet above the River Dee below.

But then, Percy would soon have to take even bigger risks in life than crossing the aqueduct. Yes, much greater risks.

NINETEEN-EIGHTEEN

I<small>T WAS</small> 1918.

The war that had broken out in the fields of Belgium and France in the summer of 1914 had by now spread to four continents and many more countries. It had been fought on land, at sea and in the air. And it had touched the lives of civilians and soldiers alike, so that no person was immune from its effects.

The war had raged as Percy had grown to a man; it was almost all he could remember. Ever since he had entered the coal mines in 1914 the unrelenting violence of the war seemed certain to destroy all that was dear to him, and never more so than in 1918. But, in his heart Percy was a boy like any other in Britain, a boy with hopes and plans, a boy who dreamed about his future with his girl.

The war rumbled on, never stopping, while Percy toiled below ground.

In 1915, there was news of the great battles at Neuve Chapelle and Loos in France, of the doomed bravery of the landings at Gallipoli, and of the eternal fights for the Belgian city of Ypres – once a Mediaeval jewel set in the mud-fields of Flanders, and now nothing more than a ruin damned by shellfire.

And then, a year later, in July 1916, there was the Somme; fierce fights for trenches, and hills, and woods; battles that saw the end for many from the land of Wales, boys whose names were now painted on the wooden crosses that appeared in thickets in the fields of Picardy.

In this way, it was the Somme that left an indelible mark on the land of Wales; for here the men of the Red Dragon, of Lloyd George's army, first saw battle in the hell that was Mametz Wood. In the depths of that wood, scarred and splintered by British guns, the Welsh fought hard to break the German trench lines. The lines held, dented and pushed, but intact; yet with persistence and not without trials, the Welshmen could still be rightly proud that they had driven the Germans from *their* wood.

The first inkling at home that the great battle had been fought was in the papers. Letters started to appear in the *Cefn Chronicle* from the soldiers who had fought there. With the summer evenings still light, Percy took to reading out the words of the soldiers to his parents. But with his mother busy with her pots, Percy had to raise his voice above the din of the clashing coppers and thick pot bowls, an echo of the violent sounds of the front.

'Now look 'ere, mam' said Percy. 'Here's one from Robbie Jones, you know, of Acrefair.' He started reading. 'Just a line to let you know I am still alive, though wounded with shrapnel in my abdomen'.

Wincing at the thought of the pain Robbie must have felt, Percy continued 'Our lot made a bayonet charge on the ——Wood and Wales may be proud of the way the RWF went through it'.

'Mam! Mam! He's talking about the lads of the Royal Welsh!' Percy knew his brothers must have been with Robbie. So he read on, even more intently.

'Just before entering the wood I was laid out; fortunately I rolled into a shell hole. It seems strange, but it was a Cefn man, who I hadn't seen since Llandudno, that helped me.'

'His name is Dai Edwards, I believe, from top Cefn'. The clashing of pots stopped abruptly. It was David. Their own David had saved a man, helped him so that the stretcher bearers could reach him.

As the light faded, and in the shadows, Ben Edwards looked away from his younger son. No, there was no room to show his emotion. Not now.

In truth, David was lucky to escape. But just as Robbie Jones had done before him, David would return, wounded, to his homeland, while so many were left behind.

With time, people became used to seeing the long lists of the missing or killed in the newspapers. They grieved equally when tragedy hit their village, their neighbourhood, their streets; but they hoped against hope that one of their own would not be amongst them.

In these papers, once hopeful pictures – the faces of boy soldiers and old sweats (as the senior soldiers were called) alike – stared out tragically from soon-fading pages under headlines 'missing in action', 'killed in the Great Push' or 'lost at sea'. And already, by 1918, almost two million men had been wounded, killed or captured – and that was in France and Belgium alone. Almost everyone knew someone who had been killed, wounded or lost.

Amongst them was Lance Corporal Hughes of Rock Terrace. Corporal Hughes who had written to the *Chronicle* to describe his trench raid. And now he was dead. '*Yr ydym i gyd yn cydymdeimlo a chwi*…we all sympathise with you' his commanding officer wrote. Just weeks ago he had written in his native Welsh to the *Cefn Chronicl*, '*Colfiwch fi* …remember me to Mrs Edwards….'

But the plain truth was there. The Somme had claimed him; another son of Cefn left lying with the other boys of the Red Dragon, in the devastated forest of Mametz, 'killed in the Great Push'.

Old Ben Edwards looked up from the paper and stared into the flame of the oil lamp. How much closer could the war get to his door?

Then, one day in November 1916, the war *did* come home to Cefn. Families with boys in the trenches could see what they saw, in moving pictures. 'The Battle of the Somme' was to be shown at The George Edwards Hall, a film that promised 'a battlefield in reality, magnificent and terrible'. Sixteen-year-old Percy could not contain his excitement.

Staring wide-eyed at the flickering images, of bustling men and bursting shells, Percy, his *tad*, and his mam saw for the first time the reality of what the older Edwards boys were facing, 'Somewhere in France'. The guns, the bayonets, the barbed wire. And when another mother cried out, 'That's my son!', a chill passed down all their spines.

Percy was horrified, and quickly tried to put thoughts of the war away. But it was not easy. The desperate eyes of the wounded men in the moving pictures haunted him.

'Perhaps we can get some chips on the way home?' he suggested, hopefully. Yes, chips. They would take their minds off the war. Plenty of salt and vinegar!

Duw, it must be tough at the front, Percy thought as be ate the soothing meal from the pages of yesterday's papers, packed with their war news. There was no escape.

Even back home in Blighty, in dear old Wales, things were getting difficult – as the war dragged remorselessly on. The *Chronicl y Cefn* still carried cheery adverts for groceries, but things were getting strained.

E. RICHARDS
Grocer and Provision Dealer

SPECIALITIES
Hams   Jams   Flour
Bacon Marmalade Bran
Cheese Tinned Goods Meal
Butter Bottled Fruits Corn

AT ROCK BOTTOM PRICES
The Gwalia Stores, Cefn

Jaunty these adverts many have been in 1916. But by 1918, with the German U-boats attacking the cargo ships on the high seas, such delights were becoming ever scarcer. Old Richards' claims were wearing thin as the shortages became more obvious.

'Rock Bottom Prices!'

Mrs Edwards was indignant. How could Mr Richards charge so much? Then there was rationing. How could she feed her family if all she was allowed was a small cube of butter? It was scandalous!

There were other changes to the face of Britain, too. In the munitions factories, on the trams, or in many, many other jobs, women had taken the place of the men who were now needed for the front. It was the case that many village girls now looked beyond their homes and looked to the factories for their future.

Old Ben Edwards had heard the rumours. The rumours that the National Shell Factory in Wrexham was paying good wages for women to work there, making munitions.

'Damn this war, it'll change everything', he'd growled under his breath to no one in particular, the other facemen nodding as they walked back from the pit.

'But if we are to win the fight, we'll need everyone we can' he said, softer this time, almost to himself.

Women soon showed they could do the work of any man, and they became freer than they had ever been. With Britain needing skilled hands and quick wits; so it was to women that the nation turned, to keep the engines running. And while women worked to make the weapons of war and to plough the fields and tend the flocks of sheep that roamed the rough Welsh hills, the nation came to rely on young men to serve in the trenches.

Now the volunteers of the early war were long gone, and now men were forced to go, come what may. And Percy was one of them. A young man of eighteen in 1918, called upon to serve. Yes, he too would take his place in the ranks.

How different it had been in the war's early days. The thousands of men of the Welsh Division, raised by Lloyd George's stirring speeches, had joined as proud volunteers. Marching gladly to serve their country, these raw Welsh boys were gradually honed into fighting soldiers. But no amount of training can take the peaceful heart of a man and forge it into a steel-hard resolve to survive battle. Only battle itself can do this.

In 1918, there was a real danger that the Germans would win the war. The world seemed less innocent, the war more cruel. As Percy scanned the *Cefn Chronicle* its very pages seemed to sigh with the names of lost boys; names that were so much at odds with the jaunty adverts for 'Hams, Jams, Flour and Bacon' of Mr Richards' grocery store.

The Germans had beaten Russia in 1917, and now thousands of battle-hardened *Frontkämpfer* – front fighters – packed the railways from the east, and flooded westwards. The might of the German eastern army was now facing the British and their allies in the west.

And so it was that in the Spring, the front fighters had attacked with such energy that a great hole appeared in the British defences. The Germans had hit at their enemy's weak points, and there was little choice for the Allies but to pull back. Terrible stories of a new defeat appeared in all the local newspapers. 'The beginning of the enemy's offensive was on a colossal scale' they reported, the day after the attack, 'he flung the full weight of a great army against us.'

A storm broke over the allied lines, and the news was grave. It became so bad that the British commander, Field Marshal Sir Douglas Haig, announced that the British armies would fight to the end, their backs against 'the wall' that was the English Channel. He would accept no failure.

As they peered at the pages of the local papers in their pit cottage, Percy's parents knew with heavy hearts that it would soon be their young son's time to serve in the army. Closing their eyes in the gloom of the pit cottage, they hoped against hope that he would still escape the horrors that had befallen their other sons on the Somme.

There was nothing else they could do. But hope.

GONE FOR A SOLDIER

By 1918, Percy had grown, and his brothers were now veterans of war. David had already been discharged, no longer a soldier. Instead, he was transformed into a wounded hero of the Somme in 1916, wearing a silver badge on his coat that bore the words 'Services Rendered. For King and Empire'.

This small token was there for *all* to see, as if his obvious limp was not sufficient; it was little enough for what *he* had seen in a battle that had consumed so many men. Yes, David had suffered, but he had survived, when so many of his pals still lay in France.

The younger Benjamin had been dealt a different card. Yes, he too was a veteran of the fearsome battles of the Somme in 1916, and of Ypres in 1917, and of sights he would never forget; but he at least had escaped unscathed, and the war had made him. Now he was a Sergeant marked by three stripes on his sleeves, equal in his eyes to any hewer from the pits of North Wales.

At home, and on leave, the miners would buy *him* a drink, singing out his name across crowds of other men.

But the Somme had just been the start of a long war journey for the Welshmen of Lloyd George's army, and there would be more battles. And there would be casualties: men killed, or who had been wounded, often terribly; men who had been taken prisoner to suffer the hardships of captivity. These losses could not be sustained if divisions like that of the Red Dragon were to carry on the fight. More and more able-bodied men would be needed to fill the gaps, and urgently.

To fill the dwindling ranks, the War Office had a solution. With losses mounting since 1915, Lloyd George had helped create an army that would face the end of the war in 1918. As the new year dawned in 1916, the Government had introduced a law that made it so that most men and boys of eighteen would have to go to war – and pit boys would be no exception.

Still posted up on the streets, even in 1918, there were early-war tattered posters that had once implored men to join up to fight – *I'r fyddin fechgyn Gwalia!* (To the Army, boys of Wales!). They were now ignored. They were ignored as no man had a choice in the matter; for now, most *had* to go to war.

Early on, the Army made it plain that only soldiers who were nineteen years of age could serve in the frontline. There had been many plucky lads who had dodged this rule, though. In 1914, while the country was in the grip of patriotic fever, taller (or cockier) boys would talk themselves into the army, swept along with the crowds, taken in by the patriotic songs, the posters – or the boasters. But this wasn't really allowed; and while many boys would serve, others would be sent home, or at least kept back from the front.

By summer 1918, the immediate threat from the German *Frontkämpfer* was over, their offensive force spent. But the German army remained a formidable foe; an army battle-hardened men, the bitter losses of those forlorn offensives replaced by the youth of the *Vaterland*.

With equally heavy casualties, every man would now be needed for the British army – even if those men were had once been just boys. Now any recruit who was eighteen and who had been trained could face the German army. Gone were the hardened soldiers with skin baked by the sun of India, Regulars of the army of Empire. No, now there was just a crop of pale new boys to fill the ranks, an army of eighteen year olds. Almost half a million more men would join in the final year of the war, half of them under nineteen.

So it was that Percy, born in a mining village to a family of coal miners, could not escape the army. He would be a soldier boy. And so, just as inevitably, would Jack.

Percy received his papers through the post in March 1918. Papers that signified that he no longer a civilian, for, Under the Military Service Act of 1916, now he reached eighteen he would be 'deemed to be enlisted for the period of the war'. The words were *very* official.

'Mam, what does "deemed to have enlisted" mean?' Percy asked while the fire danced brightly in the grate. He might be 18, but he'd always looked to his mam.

'It means you're to be a soldier, boy bach, until the King says you can come home.' His mother had known this day was approaching, but she'd hoped secretly that her young lad would not have to take his share of war.

Slowly digesting this, Percy stared intently into the kitchen fire.

A month after receiving his papers, Percy was called to his training, to make his way in the army as best he could.

Despite her brave face, Percy's mam was not ready for that. She'd seen her two older boys go to war and thanked God that both had survived the Battle of the Somme and the great fight for the wood called Mametz. And now it was Percy. Then there was Caradoc, too, the youngest boy in the house, just sixteen. Would he be called? God knows when this hated war would end.

But there was no use fretting. Instead, Mrs Edwards knew she needed to get her lad ready, to prepare him for the worst.

'Here, boy, here's some spare socks' she said, busying herself with his small parcel of belongings.

'You'll need them where you're going. Make sure they're dry, mind, before you put them on. You mark my words'.

Percy's mam had seen David's feet when he came back from the trenches. They'd suffered so, their white flesh puckered and wrinkled from constant soaking.

Mr Edwards chipped in. Quietly he pressed a matchbox in a shiny metal cover into Percy's hand.

'Son, you'll be needing this' he said, softly. Old Ben Edwards knew how much his boy liked to read the papers.

'Remember us when you light your candle'. Mr Edwards' words trailed off, barely heard by the young lad on his way to a new adventure.

In April 1918, the young recruit left Wales for Liverpool and his training camp. As Percy made his way to the railway line he passed along the green valley of the Dee. Spring was here, with the skies brightening and the birds singing as the great river flowed across its rapids, near to the town of Llangollen.

Walking to the station he paused to think of Kitty and the life he was leaving behind. Taking out his pocket-knife he carved a message into the crumbling stone walls of the railway tunnel, 'Kitty and Percy, 22nd April 1918.' He had wanted to write more, to add a message of love to those left by the *other* soldier boys for *their* best girls, and Kitty's name nestled amongst so many others.

'PRIVATE EDWARDS!' shouted the stern-faced corporal, already a veteran of the battles in France.

'Get along there, lad, we're entraining!'

Red-faced, and stepping lively to the train, Percy climbed aboard the bare third-class carriage, the corporal's voice still rich in his ears;

just for a moment that carriage reminded him of the times when as he had taken his girl on Sunday trips to the coast, and the seaside delights of Llandudno. But there was little likelihood he'd see the resort's wonderful shops, with their cast iron and glass canopies, and the salt-worn boards of the town's pier, any time soon.

And as the Dee flowed to the sea, so the boys of Wales followed its course. Reaching its estuary, the great river swept out into the dark waters of the Irish Sea, the low Welsh hills its backdrop, Liverpool in sight.

Gone for a soldier boy. Percy would swap the valley of the Dee for a valley that was not familiar. The valley of the Somme. Percy was beginning a journey that would end in France.

But first, there was the training camp – and the blast of the Sergeant-Major's voice – to survive.

SNIGGERY CAMP

O N A WINDSWEPT COAST, just north of the hustle and bustle of the Liverpool docks, was the camp. Among the patchwork of fields, and anchored into the low-lying, deep, dark earth, many huts had been built.

Sniggery was typical of so many camps that, in 1914, stretched out on any low-lying ground: countless huts to house countless soldiers. Makeshift at first, a sea of white tents muddied by the earth, these tent towns had soon been hammered into shape. And the forests of Britain had been scoured for enough wood to make huts – the women of the Forestry Corps wielding axes to provide it – to help keep the men safe, warm and dry.

Already by 1918, battalion after battalion, thousand after thousand of soldiers had lived there, slept there and trained, men destined for France. And one of those many thousands was Percy. But housing the ever-increasing numbers of young recruits that arrived daily in 1918 was a difficult task, and more often than not, tents were called upon once again to do service.

In truth, tents were not the best shelter when rain was being driven in from the Irish Sea – as Percy soon found out – but it was the best that could be done.

'The first night we got here we slept under canvas and it was raining' he wrote, to Kitty, who was safe, dry and warm in Argoed, 'our beds were fairly floating in the morning, so we had to shift from there'. He tried his best to sound hopeful, but these conditions were so typical of many camps in the last year of the war.

The Cefn lad had been called to Sniggery Camp on 23 April 1918, at the age of eighteen years and two months. He had been a pit boy,

yes, serving in the mines, but even that job had not kept him from the army. The government had drawn a comb through every work place made sure that everyone who could be a soldier would be picked out from the workers, no one left behind. And its teeth had bitten deeply into the mines, the factories and the high streets of Britain.

Percy the recruit stood just five feet 2¼ inches tall, and was just over seven stones in weight. Though a miner, he had not yet developed the iron-hard muscles of the hewer, his records showing his physical development as 'poor'. Poor, maybe; but it was obvious that Britain needed every man it could get. And Percy would surely improve with good food and hard training.

Sniggery Camp was home to the 3rd Battalion, South Wales Borderers in 1918. It was a Welsh battalion of a thousand men, and one that usually recruited in the south, far from Cefn. But where a man came from didn't worry the army, always in need of recruits – and never more so than in the last year of the war.

At night, in the gloom, a mixture of voices – sing-song mixing with the nasal tones of the north – echoed around the huts, the lyrical tones of their green land. The Welsh boys came to this camp to take part in the protection of the great port of Liverpool. But it was there also to train up the young men who were coming into the army for the first time.

Arrival at the camp was always a challenge for the boys of eighteen in 1918. Many had never been away from home – certainly Percy had never strayed from the land of Wales.

If they were at all nervous, the corporal showed little sign that he would improve their confidence. No, he'd seen sights at the front that haunted him at night, terrible sights of broken men and horses, and of the murder of the very Earth. But he kept those thoughts tightly bound up in his closely fitting khaki, and turned his attention to the youths in front of him.

'EDWARDS!' he shouted. 'WHAT ARE YOU PLAYING AT?' Percy had no idea what he was supposed to do, and had strayed from the other new lads who arrived at the windswept and care-worn camp.

'REPORT TO THE QUARTERMASTER AND RECEIVE YOUR ISSUE!'

Percy hurried along under the glare of the older man and nervously gathered up his kit. It was a mountain of gear: of scratchy khaki uniform; of stiff cotton straps, bags and pouches that had to be beaten into shape, and with brass buckles to be polished so brightly; of sundries and necessaries as the army called them – the knives and forks, brushes for all purposes, and the purposeful-looking shaving razor that Percy had, in reality, very little use for.

And it was to the armourer that the Pit Boy reported to receive his weapon of war, a rifle that he would polish, strip, oil and clean; a rifle that he would swear to look after, just as he would expect it to look after him in battle. But there was no time to think of such heroic deeds, just then. There were more mundane matters in hand, and he had to report to his hut.

The camps were rough, just timber outside and in, with simple trestles and planks for beds, and with a thin mattress on top. No home comforts, or the cosiness of a pit cottage; just a plain table and a pot-bellied, cast-iron stove to take the chill off the cold air of each wooden hut.

Nevertheless, Percy shivered in the cold. Lying awake at night he heard the sobs of the boys who had never been away from home. Lying beneath his thin blanket Percy's thoughts were of the pit cottage, of warm bakestones, of his trusty bicycle, of Jack who he knew would soon be called to the army; but most of all, of his girl, Kitty.

Even the food of the camp was roughly prepared and unpleasant; home cooking was soon to become a distant memory to the new lads of the huts. For Percy, it was a long way from his mam's warming stews and baked delights.

Percy took his place at one of the rough wooden trestle tables set up in the large mess hut. He'd collected two meagre rashers of bacon, and on each table were large white basins filled with tea from a bucket, and great hunks of rough bread; not even in the pit canteen had Percy seen such sights.

'Hi, watch it, boy bach!' shouted his neighbour, as Percy reached for his bread and nearly upset the trestle; he'd soon learned to be quick to grab a piece before they vanished. But the food was poor fare indeed.

'I am writing these few lines after breakfast' wrote Percy to his girl, 'it was a meal enough to make one sick after coming from home'. He really meant what he said.

The army cooks had many to feed in that camp of thousands. While the boys grumbled about their meal, the cooks had the next one to prepare. The recruits would grumble again when they were faced with the less-than-lean meat, stewed cabbage and overdone potatoes they'd be served that evening.

But the cooks were used to complaints.

'I'd like to see those infantry boys slaving over a Dixie cooker,' the sweating sergeant-cook muttered under his breath.

Re-adjusting to this new life was a challenge for all the boys – even though many had had a hard life in the pits, or working the land. It was a worrying time.

'Well, I have settled down to my new life alright, because it's no use breaking your heart here', Percy wrote to his sweetheart on his arrival, perhaps close to tears, even in this world of men.

He would not be alone. Many of the lads would fear the future, with heavy hearts.

The camp had been named after a small farm and wood that still nestle today in the same windswept landscape; though now there is nothing much to mark its place, the land returned to peace. Though close to Liverpool, the land of Sniggery was nonetheless rural, its rich earth perfect for farming. But with the need for men, this earth had to be given up to nurturing a new crop of soldiers, not of wheat.

Percy and Kitty had met in the beautiful Dee Valley, amongst a similar patchwork of green fields. The Dee was very important to them – and often, lying on his hard bunk in the camp, Percy would think of their times together along the magical river. 'I am glad to hear that you have a grand some times but I wish I were with you along the river', he wrote. Percy did not begrudge Kitty having fun without him, how could he? But he missed her so. And the Dee would remain close to both of them, deep in their thoughts.

Sniggery was tantalisingly close to Liverpool – and given a free day, if he wished, Percy could cross the Mersey for a sight of the Dee and Wales beyond. But there were other attractions too. Nearby, bordering the low fields, was a belt of sand-dunes with an expanse of golden sand beyond. The beach was perfect for training runs and exercise, where once laughing children had played with bucket and spade. From the dunes the boys could watch the ships as they plied into one of Britain's most important ports, each one of them packed with valuable goods from America, each one vital for Britain's survival.

It was also a perfect spot for the new soldiers to step out in their new clothes. Barely fitting, stiff and itchy, the tough woollen cloth and unyielding boots of the soldier's uniform were designed to hold up to rough treatment in the trenches. Despite this, making the change from flat cap and pit boots was perhaps not so difficult for the miners and countrymen from Wales. With their uniforms finished off with puttees, the peculiar 'bandages' of cloth that were wound around the legs to protect them, a military cap, and a wide belt with polished brasses, each new recruit may well have felt a new pride.

In honesty, perhaps, with *too* much pride, for the boys could walk taller on the promenade that bordered the sea and dunes, taking in admiring glances from the bright young ladies of Liverpool.

'We went to a place called Seaforth last night for a walk' wrote Percy to Kitty, 'It's a very pretty place but don't go and think I went after girls'. (Secretly, Percy was proud of his new khaki.)

Yet, despite all the attention, Kitty's soldier boy was still true to his girl who worked in the dark cellars of Argoed Hall, high above the Dee. And to prove it, he nervously signed his letters T.O.I.L. – To the One I Love.

Settled into the camp, there was the serious work to be done for the new recruits. With the Germans pressing the Allies hard in the spring of 1918, the boys would soon have to be men.

And the only way they were going to do that was through training. Training, and more training.

IN TRAINING

WHEN THE BRITISH ARMY WENT TO WAR in 1914, the official manuals were very clear. Every man would need a full nine months of training before he could call himself a soldier.

But by 1918, with so many casualties from the long years of war, gaps had started to appear in the ranks; gaps that could not easily be filled. Replacement soldiers were hard to come by. And nine months was a long time to wait for them so that the army could grow to full strength.

There was danger too, for with the German army reinforced by hardened soldiers from the east, they were ready to attack. There was real danger that the British army would not be able to hold them back.

No; the nine months training would have to be reduced. More men were needed, even if those men were just boys of eighteen.

Percy saw just four months before he went to France. It seemed long enough for the slight pit boy from Cefn, trying his best to live up to the khaki uniform he now wore. But in truth, four months was little preparation for a soldier to face the might of the German army, a military machine intent on ending the war, at all costs.

Percy wasn't daunted. For now, at any rate. He would do his bit.

Lying on his hard barrack bed one June evening, he picked up his copy-ink pencil, and began to compose a letter to his sweetheart.

'Cheer up dear' wrote Percy to Kitty, 'once my training will be finished I'll be able to come home very often – unless they send me to France'. (Maybe, he thought, it would be all over soon?) The June sky was still bright, and Percy was feeling cheerful. He pasted down the letter flap, determined to give it to the postal corporal in the morning.

'Perhaps he won't have to go?' thought Kitty, as she read the letter just a day later; and hoping against hope, she willed the war to end. But she knew, deep down, that this was not to be. Percy would take his place in the line. The long line of soldiers who marched towards the trenches.

Shivering on his bunk in the cool of the Sniggery air, Percy knew that he had to learn to be a soldier from scratch. All that he'd learnt in the deep pits of Ruabon, with its dark dangers, was not sufficient to make him a soldier alone.

He had already been given his uniform; but a khaki suit does not make a soldier, especially when just tying his puttees was a challenge for even the smartest soldier, the long woollen cloth strips becoming hopelessly tangled. And that was not all; Percy had to learn how to buckle on his equipment, and to understand regulations that told him where to place all the many things a soldier needed to carry into battle. For a lad who had so few possessions, it was a bewildering mountain of military stuff.

In truth, though, the only *things* that mattered to Percy were his few personal items, objects that he kept close to him at all times. Those prized possessions were protected and cared for: letters and battered photographs of his family kept folded into a worn wallet; his bible from the Chapel, with all its hope; his wristwatch with its luminous dial that had guided him so many times on his trips to meet Kitty; yes, these were all he valued. But perhaps most of all there was the special matchbox cover his father had given him, an unspoken bond between the gruff pitman and his son.

Percy knew what light meant to men like his father, and its importance in the gloom of the coal pits, the carefully lit safety lanterns leading their way. And he knew that this simple token was a remembrance of the pits, and of his family, the gift of light to guide him at the front, a lit candle for his father. This was the special gift of his *Tada*, the hewer of coal. And it would never leave him.

'48840 EDWARDS!' shouted the corporal, 'WHAT ARE YOU PLAYING AT?' it was to his military equipment – and the mess that Percy had made of it – that the drill corporal's attention was turned (and with so many Welsh boys, it was no wonder he used Percy's number).

'YOU HAVE NO IDEA WHAT YOU ARE DOING, LAD!' There was no doubt that Percy was bewildered by the new kit. Nervously, he fumbled with its straps under the fierce glare of his corporal.

Its official name, 'Pattern 1908 Web Infantry Equipment', was a little terrifying to the new boy from Cefn. Made up of a tangle of heavy cotton straps and pouches with brass buckles, his kit took practice to assemble. And the army insisted that *every* inch of it would have to be cleaned, polished and looked after.

'I spend my time cleaning brasses,' Percy wrote to Kitty, his hands sore from the rubbing, from the constant dipping of the cloth into his tin of 'Soldier's Friend' cleaning paste, and of the relentless brushing. He knew that if there was *even* a speck of dirt, he would be in trouble.

Once the equipment was assembled, and fully packed, it was heavy – as heavy as two-thirds of Percy's bodyweight. Though the pit boy knew what it was like to haul coal, this was something different; he would have to run with the dead weight of the kit, strapped tightly to his back and chest. Yes, training was going to be tough, very tough for a lad who the army doctors had said was under-height and under-weight. There was much to learn, and lots to endure.

To build Percy up, every day there was exercise. There were 'physical jerks', to strengthen his body; and runs, to build up his stamina. These became harder and harder as the days passed. Exhausted, after the bugles had sounded 'lights out', Percy would fall onto his trestle bed and sleep the sleep of the dead – while all around him the snores of the young soldiers cut into the stillness. He never noticed.

Before he could leave his homeland, each soldier had to be protected against disease, and typhoid – a deadly fever caused by infected water that was so common in war zones – was most feared by the army. He would have to be inoculated, vaccinated, before he could go overseas. In truth, it was the effects of the vaccination itself that most soldiers were frightened of, not the disease.

'We have all been vaccinated,' he wrote to Kitty, one day at Sniggery.

'The chaps are fainting when they are on parade, but they don't get much sympathy here'.

The Drill Sergeant had seen it all before.

'They're just lads' he thought, 'just boys'. But it was not his job to worry about them. They had a job to do. If he could not harden them now, how would they fare at the front?

'CORPORAL! TAKE THAT MAN'S NAME!' he shouted, as Percy's chum stumbled in the line. Percy was among the lucky ones.

'I have stuck it so far', wrote Percy to his Kitty, 'but it hasn't affected me so bad, and some chaps' arms have swollen so much, that you can't see the shape of their elbows.' He had escaped lightly – but it meant that he had no choice but to keep on with his training. He had no chance of being 'excused duty'.

Percy's training continued on the windswept and lonely beaches and patchworks of damp fields north of Liverpool. As he and the other Welsh boys exercised they were buffeted by the stiff air sweeping in gusts from the Irish Sea.

Here, in the open fields of Lancashire, Percy and his comrades were getting fitter. The life-giving sun's rays were playing on their skin, browning the fair complexions of these boys from Wales. Percy was getting sunburned – for he was no longer working his day in the depths of the Welsh hills, in the pits where no natural light penetrated, and from which he would often emerge, blinking, into the summer daylight.

Percy was being transformed. And as new, fresh-faced, and worried recruits arrived, the tanned faces of the now-experienced ones must have struck awe into them. For, even with all their youth, these were now the 'trained men,' those next in line for France. Percy would surely have felt proud as he saw the newest boys struggle with their puttees, as he had done before them, not so very long ago.

The now-bronzed recruits often posed for photos. Local photographers came from Liverpool to set their heavy wooden and brass cameras on large tripods, and the lads would pose, one by one, or in small groups. Most of them looked painfully young in those photographs, just eighteen years of age.

'A man came around our huts asking us to have our photo taken,' Percy wrote one day, 'so our corporal shouted us out'. 'Shouted them out' to form uncertain groups outside their huts, some smiling, some glum, others simply bemused by the paraphernalia of the civilian photographer.

Percy was not inspired by the outcome. 'Well dear I have broken another camera' (just by looking into the lens), 'me and my pal look just the same as if we were going into a charge'. Obviously, getting their expressions just right was harder than expected. These photographs, so easily taken, so cheaply produced, would become so precious in the months ahead.

Percy carefully placed his pictures in envelopes, letters to carry the image of a soldier boy to the pit cottage in Cefn, and to the servant's quarters of Argoed Hall.

As the weeks went by, so Percy's confidence as a soldier grew. He went on 'manoeuvres' with the other young soldiers, practising for the real thing, the war in France; or on 'schemes' with other recruits as the enemy – deadly play-acting in the time of war. Percy and his mates also learned how to use their rifles, weapons that could fire almost fifteen bullets a minute in the right hands. Few were capable of doing this, though, as it was hard manipulating the rifle bolt; instead, the soldier-boys would rely on deadly bombs that required little skill other than pulling a pin and throwing it at an enemy – with a cool head.

That was not all. The Welsh boys had to be ready to face gas, the poisonous cloud that would catch the unwary, released from the shells that might burst amongst them at the front. Fitting the terrible masks, gripping the mouthpieces with their teeth, Percy and his pals were forced to run through a chamber filled with the noxious fumes. It was as well that many had seen the mines, were not afraid of dark, combined spaces, so full of dust.

And then there was the bayonet. Just as the Welsh had fought the English six centuries before with swords, spears and all manner of blades, so modern soldiers had to learn how to attach their bayonet to their rifles and charge, as if warriors attacking the armoured knights of ancient times. It was a most terrifying experience.

To get their men ready for this most horrific act of war, the army instructors taught the men to scream, shout and contort their youthful faces into visions of fright. Many of the instructors were old soldiers, veterans of battle, men wounded early in the war; their scars so evident that no new soldier could easily forget his fears, or escape the inevitable. And the instructors knew that getting men to charge with the blade in training was to prepare them for the worst in France.

Percy tried his hardest to be light hearted about this most violent act. But how could he possibly share this experience with Kitty?

'You should have seen us today on bayonet fighting,' he wrote to his girl, a world apart in peaceful Vron, 'we were half mad'. 'The man who can pull the ugliest face and do the most shouting is the best, so you can think what sort of a thing it is.' Could Kitty ever imagine? (Those at home never could.)

Percy was starting to understand, though; his officers were all young men, wounded men, some with limps, or even missing limbs; evidence of battle. This was a serious matter indeed. And while Kitty was tiring of her role as a servant girl in Argoed Hall, Percy knew he had no escape from Sniggery Camp and beyond. 'You saying that you can't stick it' he wrote to her; 'well, I wish we could leave this place just like that.' He knew here was no chance of that happening soon.

'I don't think it will be long before I leave now' he wrote in August, 'but I hope not.' The reality was starting to dawn on him; he too would go to war, as so many had done before him. He would follow in the footsteps of his brothers. And he, too, would wear the Red Dragon of Wales, in the poppy fields of Flanders.

On the eve of leaving for France, Percy, wrote to his love. In his head was a jaunty song written in 1915 by two other lads from North Wales, a song that captured everything he was feeling just then, sitting in his lonely hut, thinking of home, of Wales, and of the Dee that was so precious to them both.

'Just as that song says, pack all your troubles in your old kit bag and smile'. He was putting a brave face on for his Kitty – he was trying to persuade himself that everything would be all right.

As he stuffed his own kit bag for France, he was determined to pack away those worries, and to carry on like all those who had carried on before.

TO FRANCE

E VER SINCE SNIGGERY CAMP, Percy had been trying to join his
brother Ben, and his friend Jack, in the regiment of North Wales.

Jack. Just a lad. Now, even *he* had been taken from the pit to serve
with the Red Dragon on his shoulder. He too had received 'the call',
and the army's relentless machine had taken him. There was no escape.
Now in training, Jack was a long way from his closest pal, from Percy;
for he was at Kinmel, a camp near the Welsh coast simply miles away
from his best chum.

Percy's mate from pit and village had been drafted into the Royal
Welsh Fusiliers, and this very fact wrankled him. It was his brothers'
regiment, and the regiment of the north. And now, being separated
from his closest friend, was another blow.

'I am trying to get a transfer to the R.W.F. to get to Jack,' Percy
wrote to Kitty, one warm night in July. He still had high hopes
that he would be transferred from the South Wales Borderers, his
training unit and a regiment from Brecon. After all, this was a place
that was *so* far away from his home, with Welsh voices *so* different
from his own.

'I have got two brothers in the Royal Welsh, one discharged, so I think I will stand a good chance of being transferred.' he wrote to Kitty, weighing up his chances of a move to the regiment of his dreams. Percy knew that with the Fusiliers having fought so hard at Mametz on that fateful Somme day in 1916, his brothers' exploits would allow him to boast – if only he was able to join them.

'Everything will be better if I can just be with Jack', he mused as he lay on his rough bed listening to the irregular snoring of his new comrades. Percy remembered the good times on the Dee, the darkness of the pit, and of the two boys who looked out for each other. Friends in the pit could usefully be friends in the frontline, he concluded, before turning on his side to snatch some fitful sleep.

But it was not to be; not yet, anyway. For just as Percy had been trained with the regiment of South Wales at Sniggery, so he would be sent out to join them in France.

One morning, Percy stared up at the rough notice board that announced the next drafts, the names of the men who would be going to the France, to the base camps on the other side of the English Channel, and then to the Front. He knew that there was no chance that he would join the bold body of North Welshmen that had already gathered fame, with six Victoria Crosses awarded for utmost valour in battle in this long war, and with more to come.

No, he would have to stay with the Borderers. For in 1918, with the situation in France grave, all men were wanted; there was no time for niceties.

'No matter', he thought, as he packed his kit and prepared himself for the journey. So be it. If he wasn't to be with his best friend, at least he would be with all the lads he'd trained with in the desolate fields and storm-lashed beaches of Sniggery.

Leaving the camp, the new soldiers of the draft for France made their way from Liverpool Lime Street to the channel coast. It was a regular occurrence for the people of that proud city, and few passers-by looked up as yet another crowd of soldier boys thronged the station.

At Lime Street, smoke from the deeply blackened engines pervaded the atmosphere, and there were great gusts of steam as the mighty locomotives drew out, the line deep-cut through coarse stone so similar to that of Cefn, and of home.

Percy looked up at the great cast iron arches of the station that were a far cry from the cosy waiting rooms of the local railway line at Ruabon. Instead, they had much in common with the cast iron beams and begrimed lifting gear that drew the coal from the pits so close to his village.

Picked out on the great platforms, there were knots of women who weaved between the khaki-clad boys of eighteen. Many of them were mothers. And there were intense scenes enough to remind travellers and passers-by of the emotional dramas of flag-waving in 1914.

But this was 1918, and the mood was more sombre; for after years of cruel war, the mothers had witnessed too much to make it seem like a noble crusade, even though the Red Dragon was everywhere on the shoulders of their soldier-boys, with its echoes of a chivalric past.

Secretly, the women on the platform had prayed that the war would be over by now, and that their sons would be spared, what with the war so advanced. But the German spring attacks had hit hard like a hammer against metal, and those blows had meant that their boys would be next in line to resist them. There was little the mothers could do, but wave their sons on their way, heavy-hearted, but still retaining hope, always hope.

Here and there at Lime Street, there were younger, fresher faces that peered out with bright, tear-rimmed eyes from beneath jaunty hats and bonnets. Handkerchiefs tightly grasped, the sweethearts stood awkwardly by as their boys were gathered together by sergeants and corporals, ready to get on board the long line of carriages that formed the troop-train bound eventually for Folkestone.

For Percy, there was little chance *his* sweetheart could be there to bid him *bon chance*. She was needed at Argoed and, after all, it was *such* a journey to Liverpool. Percy wrote to Kitty with a heavy heart, 'I think it will be a long while before we meet again, but I hope it will come very soon.' He hesitated as he wrote this time.

'At least she's with Gertie', thought Percy as he boarded the troopship, the train having reached its south coast destination. He knew that Kitty's best friend would comfort her in the times when the Hall fell quiet, when there was time to dwell on what might become, and to fear the worst.

Now crossing the Channel, with England fading behind him, the pit-boy soldier thought of the two girls, of the darkness of the cellars at Argoed, of the dizzying heights of the old aqueduct, and of the four of them, Percy and Kitty, Jack and Gertie, swinging through the streets of Llangollen to the rapids of the Dee, the river roaring as it passed on over the rocks downstream.

'The Dee will still keep flowing, whatever happens', he mused. And it made him ready to meet his next challenge. For whatever *did* happen, Kitty would still be there, waiting.

The troopship docked at Boulogne, and for Percy at least, it was exciting just to be in France.

'I had a very pleasant journey across the water. I think we have settled down for a while now, well I hope so anyhow,' wrote Percy to Kitty. Percy had never been on a ship before.

By water, he meant the English Channel, that strip of sea that stood between Britain and the rest of the continent of Europe. A pleasant journey. Percy was being brave, for on that trip he and his mates had peered out to sea pensively, fearful of seeing a streak of boiling water that might mark the track of a torpedo. Nonetheless, his arrival was the moment that Percy had been waiting for.

Yes, he put aside fears of those German submarines lurking in the depths, and had braced himself against the rail of the ship, his face turned towards France, a new land, and a new life.

AT THE BASE

Percy's training had prepared him to be a soldier: but in truth nothing could prepare him for what was to come.

As he arrived at Boulogne, Percy was suddenly thrust into a new world. Everywhere there were men in khaki. As they spoke, the Tommies produced a gaggle of rich dialects from all corners of Britain. Welsh boys stood out from those from the mill towns of Yorkshire, the docks of Belfast, Birkenhead or Glasgow, or from those Cockney men born within sound of the Bow Bells.

French words must have come hard to a young lad from Cefn, a lad with Welsh in his soul; and as the gaggle of children gathered around the new arrivals, pressing them for souvenirs, for bully beef or biscuits, the din must have been overwhelming. Nevertheless, hungry, the men sought help in battered phrasebooks that advised soldiers to repeat, haltingly, 'Don-nay mwa ah man-jay, sil-voo-play?' Can I have some food, please?

(The French were used to the British by now. They would get their food, no matter *how badly* the soldiers pronounced their language. They owed them that.)

From the port the boys were marched to their new camp, an Infantry Base Depot. Here, every day, the young soldiers were hardened with a view to war. The camps of huts and tents stretched along the French coast, sprawling with an intensity born out of necessity. For if the allies were to win the war, they would need men and more men, to face the massing *Frontkämpfer*.

Percy knew that his time for the trenches was close.

He knew that he had to let Kitty know he was safe – so he took one of the peculiar postcards from the bunch the corporal had in his hand, and read the instructions carefully.

'Field Service Post Card. NOTHING is to be written on this side except the date and signature of the sender. <u>If anything else is added the postcard will be destroyed</u>.'

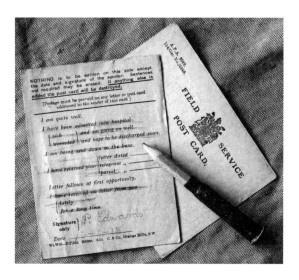

Taking the underlining seriously, nervously, Percy crossed out those pre-prepared sentences that did not apply: 'I have been admitted to hospital', and 'I am being sent down to the base'. He wondered at their meaning as he licked his pencil. All he was left with was the line: 'I am quite well. Letter follows at the first opportunity'. Kitty would be worried, nevertheless.

'Still, it's better than nothing' he thought, as he thrust the addressed card into the box. He knew that it wouldn't be long before he wrote to Kitty, now as a plucky soldier lad in France, the same as all the other plucky lads.

'Just a brief note to let you know that I am in the pink, hoping you are the same.' He wrote, in his first full letter home from the base camp.

'In the Pink' – there it was again, that casual phrase: 'I'm fine, don't worry'. The officer checking the soldiers' letters for carelessly revealed secrets had read that line a thousand times. Looking up from his work, the Lieutenant must have wondered how long the new soldiers would remain that way. In the Pink.

And so it was that the new boys worked hard to improve their soldiering. They had learned the basics at Sniggery, but at the Base Camp they needed to harden themselves to the demands of the soldier's life at the front. In the sand dunes of France – just as they had in the dunes of Lancashire – the boys learned what it was like to face the enemy. Here, on a vast sandy training ground known as the 'bull ring', hard men with stripes on their sleeves and with even harder voices worked to make the boys fit to face the steel-helmeted might of the German army.

In those sand dunes of France, the young soldier boys worked tirelessly to become better soldiers, and all thoughts of the coal mines of Ruabon moved to the back of their minds.

The Welsh boys ran with full equipment until they felt like they could never run again. They learned how to put on their gas masks and to throw grenades. They stuck their bayonets into sacks of yielding straw. And they were issued with their one-hundred and twenty bullet cartridges; real, live bullets, for the first time. Those bullets felt heavy as the young soldiers packed them, with nervous fingers, into their equipment. They were certainly a weighty responsibility.

And as each day passed, the boys of the base knew the time would come when they would have to move up to the front, when they would have to take the place of those who had given their lives for their country.

'Some of my pals are going home on draft leave tomorrow,' Percy wrote, one day, from his hut, 'how I wish I were going with them.' His thoughts were with Kitty, and with the land that the soldiers called 'Blighty'.

At the front, and moving into the line, was the division of the Red Dragon; numbered the 38th, it was some 16,000 men of Lloyd George's army. As it had done on the Somme in 1916, so once more the Welsh division prepared to take its place in history, to help drive back the enemy. But such times at the front had been costly. Soon the boys of the 38th would need help, more men, more replacements from the base depots.

Percy was now to be one of them (and Jack would be next). His time had come. And more; he found that he was to join the Royal Welsh Fusiliers after all, and to move to the front, to the sound of the guns, to the trenches, to the frontline.

Boarding a troop train, Percy and the other new boys of the RWF stared with disbelief at the sign that said 'Hommes 40, Chevaux 8', wondering whether it did *really* mean that forty men and eight horses were to be packed into the small space together.

The boys took their place in the truck and watched from the open door as the train set off from the green pastures of France to the ancient city of Amiens. The loaded train was painfully slow, much slower than the mine trucks he had so often served below ground. It was up to the soldiers to find ways of breaking the tedium as they clacked slowly towards the battlefront. They sang, they chatted, and stared with curiosity at the women tending the fields, many of them garbed in black.

Often, they jumped down from the train when it ground to a halt, brakes squealing, trucks clanking.

'Hi! HI!' Percy shouted as he ran alongside the chattering carriages. He was shouting to the *chef de train*.

'Hi! Monsieur? Water! Eau?'

It was easy for the driver and brakemen to keep '*les Tommees*' happy. Climbing down from the cabin they filled Percy's outstretched tin with hot water, that precious liquid that would ensure the Welsh boys would get their *paned o de*, their cup of tea. Very soon that tea would be like nectar to the boys in the trenches, but here they could savour it, made from the very water, the steam, that was driving them to the front.

Onwards, they travelled from the ancient – now war-scarred – city of Amiens, the boys went go up the line to the front, the sound of the guns increasing with every mile travelled. Low booms at first, as if the distant thunder that Percy had once heard sweep across the rugged landscape of Wales, accompanied by a storm of heavy raindrops that crashed down on slate tiles of the cottage in good old Rock Place. But soon those booms increased in intensity, and instead of raindrops, there came a storm of steel.

From beneath his heavy helmet, Percy pulled his collar up to guard against shivers as he marched, making his way to the trenches, those dirty ditches from which the nations had waged war for four whole years.

Even the summer evenings could be cool in the wounded fields of France.

UP THE LINE

THE SOMME HAD SEEN MUCH FIGHTING in this war.

In better days it had been a beautiful part of France, a green land of soft rolling hills, of the beautiful sounds of the skylarks ascending to sing their ancient song; of angular plots of trees, and of small villages reached by narrow roads worn down into the soft white chalk beneath. Through this land the River Somme – so like that of the Dee – flowed with intent to reach the coast, and the smaller Ancre joined it, through a valley choked with wildlife. Above, the vast summer skies were so blue that it seemed almost impossible to be true.

But in the summer of 1916, those vast skies had been reduced to a soldier's eye view, a slot-like view, a view from up inside a trench, cut deeply into the glaring white chalk. The same blue skies were rent by screaming shells that discharged death to landscape and men alike. The villages were destroyed, the rivers polluted, the ground broken by countless shell holes.

Like his brothers, two years before him, Percy was destined to see this Somme, this wounded land.

With his family's history, and with so many boys from Cefn in the ranks of the good old Royal Welsh, it was a matter of great pride for Percy when he was finally drafted into its ranks. 'I have been transferred to the RWF.' he wrote, glowing with the thought, to his best girl, 'there was about two hundred of us transferred'. Percy had finally been drafted into the 17th Royal Welsh Fusiliers, a unit first formed in answer to Lord Kitchener's call for 'men and more men' in 1914.

The 17th Battalion, a thousand good men, had been raised from volunteers in seaside Llandudno, that great beauty so popular with holidaymakers. It was a place that, in times of peace, called out to Kitty and Percy, Jack and Gertie, who escaped to it when they could, on snatched day trips, their feet bare on amongst the sands and multi-coloured pebbles of the beach. Leaving behind the industry of Cefn, and the confines of Argoed, the four friends took sweet ices on the grand pier that stretched out into the Irish Sea. Perhaps when peace came they could once more chase their dreams at the seaside?

But in 1914, in place of fine summer hats and light airs from bandstands, the promenade had been filled with khaki caps, and with the cries of corporals fussing over regulations.

By now, in 1918, the local Battalion had long since lost its local feel. All comers were welcome, and needed, to join its number; men who no longer came to Llandudno to fill the empty rooms of the lodging houses but who instead were drafted in to fill the empty spaces of the ranks, left by the months of battle. These men would see France and the battlefront soon enough.

In August 1918, the boys of the 17th Royal Welsh Fusiliers were once again close to Mametz, the wood of legend for every Welshman.

Oh, how it had changed. In July 1916, the wood had been a living, breathing, entity; a green haven for wildlife. Dappled light had penetrated through the tree cover and played on the ground

below. Facing it, the Welshmen of 1916 had no idea what the wood contained. Ten men or ten thousand, *Deutscher soldaten*, there was no way of knowing. They soon found out. As the gallant Welsh charged the wood, they were cut down by the Germans it concealed.

The stretcher-bearers had picked up David Edwards from the torn wood that fateful day in July.

'Don't worry, bach', they said, 'we've got you. You're safe now.'

From a haze of pain, Percy's brother could see the grubby white bands on their arms with the blood-red letters SB, and was thankful that there were brave men willing to face the guns with nothing but armbands and bandages.

Percy well remembered the official envelope that arrived in the aftermath of that terrible battle, one afternoon in July 1916. He remembered how his mam had sunk to the ground clutching the brown envelope tightly. So many boys would not be coming back to the hills of Wales.

'Regret to inform you…' the letter started, 'that Pte Edwards was wounded in action…'. *Diolch I Duw*…Thank God… he would be coming home. Percy hoped his mother would never again have to receive a letter like it.

Now, in 1918, the wood had more secrets to reveal – but it was no longer a wood. It was the place where a wood had been, a wreck of splinters, a waste of shell holes. And it was once more in the frontline, following the German spring successes of 1918. Then, in April, the might of the Kaiser's army had punched through the Allies and had threatened them with defeat; all of the hard-won gains of two years ago were left behind as the Allies retreated. The line had been held, but at great cost.

Months later, fortunes changed.

On 8 August 1918, the allied armies had started the long battle at Amiens that would rage for one hundred days, a battle that would push the Germans back and back until the war was ended.

The commander of the British army in France, Field Marshal Sir Douglas Haig, was known to be a serious man. As he rose from his bed early on the day that changed the face of the war, he took in the air.

'Fine night and morning' the Field Marshal jotted down in his diary, though noticing there was a 'slight mist in the valley'. Haig was confident he had put all the plans in place. An all-out attack would push the Germans back, and it had worked. The Germans were withdrawing.

'Who would have believed this possible even two months ago?' Haig smiled at the thought of it. Was the end of the war in the air?

But his enemy was not done yet.

Percy stepped into this battle twenty days later. The British army and its allies was advancing. But at every step, the German army was standing in the way. And at one small part of the front, facing the might of the still-powerful German war machine, was the fresh-faced youth of Wales.

'Dear Kitty', Percy wrote, one day from France, 'I have been up the line, and have now come back to the base for a rest'. His letter said much by telling little. What must he have seen? What terrors had he experienced? Sights of blackening bodies and the wanton destruction, of the worst that men could do to other men.

He could not say. He would not say.

In any case, he would soon be back in the thick of it. There was no turning back. He would join the war's final battles; he would fight against the most formidable odds.

It was all he could do.

THE TRENCHES

Pᴇʀᴄʏ'ꜱ ꜰɪʀꜱᴛ ᴇxᴘᴇʀɪᴇɴᴄᴇ ᴏꜰ ᴛʀᴇɴᴄʜ ᴡᴀʀꜰᴀʀᴇ was nothing like that his brothers had endured in 1916.

Then, there had been robustly built trenches, dug-outs for shelter, and strong-points with machine guns. Then, there had been a set routine of sentries at night, and of times – in the early morning and at dusk – when the *Soldaten* would have to 'stand to' with their rifles, ready to stop an enemy foolish enough to venture across into the teeth of well-armed men and rattling machine guns. Even deep in the trench itself, death could come at any moment.

One day in 1916, Percy picked out a letter in the *Chronicle* from Will Wilkes, a good friend of the boys, that said it all; a letter that told of an average day in an average trench in the front line, in the middle of the war.

'It was on Sunday. We all had orders to stand to arms, and at the same time we were waiting to be relieved, as we had just finished four days in the trenches.'

Four days of intense concentration, Four nights without sleep. Four average days 'in the trenches'. The letter continued.

'There were ten of us together. We were all singing some good old Welsh hymns when very suddenly a shell fell in the midst of us.' Percy read on.

'The shell killed four right on the spot, and wounded four others. I thank God that I am alive to tell the tale'.

Will Wilkes had been saved by his *Beibl*, the holy book stopping a piece of shrapnel. Percy vowed that *he too* would carry a *Beibl* if *he* was ever called to serve.

Now, in 1918, the trenches were little more than disused ditches, abandoned lines left behind by both armies as they moved across the old battlefield of 1916. Percy patted his uniform pocket. Yes, *his* holy book was still there.

The war had changed. Even in the short time that Percy had been in the trenches, the boys of Wales had been pressing hard at the Germans to their front. By early September, Mametz had been left far behind as the 38th Division pushed onwards towards the *Siegfried Stellung*, a fortress of deep trenches, formidable and unforgiving forests of barbed wire, and deep obstacles like the swift flowing Canal du Nord. These would have to be crossed, breached, if the Germans could be expelled from France, and the war brought to its end.

But for now, each battle to achieve this dream was fought with the utmost ferocity, with whirlwind bombardments and mechanical monsters moving across the tortured landscape. The old trenches of 1916 were once more held by men, fought over; but now, in 1918, more often than not they would serve only as a place to resist, or from which to launch an attack.

For Percy, it was an exhilarating experience to be involved in a real battle for the first time. After all the training, and the suspense of wondering, it was almost a relief.

'I have had no time to write' he explained to Kitty, breathlessly, in early September, while he was away from the front, 'because we have been after old Fritz, who's been retiring ever since we went into

the line. We followed him up for about six miles and he kept running away all the time', he wrote, excitedly. There was surely hope he would see Kitty and Cefn again soon.

It would be over soon!

The shock of the exploding shells was terrific. Some would arrive without warning, whizz-BANG!, exploding with a sharp retort and sending deadly metal splinters spinning through the air. Others seemed to burst in the air with a cloud of smoke, yet delivering a load of deadly balls that would cut through everything in its path. And then there was the rumbling detonation of the biggest shells, crruuMMP! These would knock the breath from any man safely in a trench, and would deliver deadly jagged steel fragments a foot long.

This lightning war was intense.

And Percy was in the middle of it. How could he ever hope to describe the war in a way that could be understood in a peaceful valley in North Wales? He couldn't. Instead he stuck to the facts. 'Fritz caught a few of our chaps with his artillery, and our artillery knocked many of his out,' he wrote on 10 September 1918. In this attack, two officers and thirty other soldiers were either killed or wounded. How else could he explain it to his people at home?

The sight was something he could never have imagined.

Percy had often wondered whether he would be able to stomach the war, to endure what so many other boys, equally ill-prepared, had done before him. But it was the sheer anger of the guns that he could never describe. Unexpected power unleashed on still innocent bodies.

No, Percy vowed to keep that to himself. And if he was ever to be reunited with Kitty, with Jack and Gertie, he would brush aside the sound of the shrieking shells and allow the insistent cries of the seagulls to replace it. (If he was ever to get back).

Percy looked up from his thoughts and shouldered his heavy equipment and rifle. Fritz was on the run! And it was the boys of the 17th RWF who were pushing him, driving the Germans back before them, across a landscape that had already had its fill of war.

Here, near the Somme village of Lechelle, the landscape rolled like breakers on a beach. The attacking armies took the chance to blend into its dips to protect themselves from the metal showers that lashed the land, the men in its shelter. The rich soil of France, normally a deep nut-brown, ready to nurture crops, was now stained by the brutality of war and was choked with its debris. The country boys amongst the Welsh miners must have wondered if it would ever yield crops again.

For Percy and the other boys just eighteen years old, the fatigue of battle was starting to tell. The dark pits of Wales had held many dangers, of roof collapses or of explosions from gasses built up in their depths; and death was never far away in the mines. Yet even these tragedies, striking to the heart of the tight-knit communities, could not prepare the young miner-soldiers for what was ahead of them.

On the other side of the barbed wire, the German troops were battle hardened. They had seen much war in Russia and France, and they were ready to defend *Vaterland und Heimat* – Fatherland and home – from their enemies, at all cost. Their belt buckles carried the slogan *Gott mit Uns* – God with us. This belief, and the knowledge that they were protecting all that was dear to them, meant these German boys were not yet ready to lay down their arms. No, they would fight to the end. And the special attack soldiers, *Sturmtruppen*, were still ready to deliver a storm on the British lines, a time when the German eagle would have to face the Welsh dragon in battle.

In the once abandoned trenches in front of Lechelle, Percy and his mates of the 17th occupied the line. The pit boy from Cefn had been in the trenches for two weeks, and he had experienced it all, and seen sights he could never unsee.

On 12 September 1918, orders were received: '17th RWF to push out patrols to ascertain if enemy frontline is held or not'. At night, raiders would go out stealthily, crawling out into the gloom to test the strength of the enemy, or to bring back prisoners through the darkness. The enemy lines were held; they resisted the intrusion, and eighteen men were killed or wounded.

Percy, on duty in that wrecked old trench that night, strained his eyes as he sought out the shadowy shapes in the black night, trying to tell friend from foe. His beloved wristwatch glowed in the night sky, his link with Kitty and home. How he wished he was back in Wales, on his bike – chancing his arm by riding over the Pontyscyllite Aqueduct to reach his girl. And, all the while, he gained comfort from her letters, so tightly bound together in their wallet, and stuffed into his uniform pocket. As the raiders returned, he shouted his challenge:

'HALT! Who goes there!' he shouted, falteringly at first, just as the corporal had taught him at Sniggery.

'Relax, pal, it's the 17th!'.

No Fritz could sing out a reply like a boy from Wales.

All was well, and Percy could rest easy.

TRENCH RAID

'LECHELLE, 13 SEPTEMBER 1918. 9.50 AM Enemy barrage opened on the whole battalion front'.

It was all very matter-of-fact. Every battalion while at the front had to keep a record of their actions, and the 17th RWF was no different. Lieutenant-Colonel Beasley had passed the task to one of his other officers, who licked the end of his blunt permanent pencil, while sheltering from the shells that roared over his head. But in filling out 'Army Form C.2118' while his candle stuttered in the breeze, he was putting off an even more terrible task.

What could he say to the families who had lost their sons in battle? The patrols of the night before had been so costly, and there was much to be done after this day of bombardment. His notes mapped out the day in four lines only; a day that was to change the streets of Cefn forever.

The day had begun with the Welsh trench-soldiers finishing their usual morning routine. Through strained eyes the boys had surveyed their front, grateful that the dawn had come without trouble, beautiful and still, and marked with bright autumn sunshine that helped warm their already trench-worn bodies. But tired as they were, they made sure they did not put their heads above parapet – that would be foolish. The snipers took aim at any helmet that showed itself.

The night before had been terrible, but at least they knew that there were enemy soldiers in the trenches ahead. They would have to be careful, because in them there were German *Sturmtruppen* who were not going to give up their positions lightly. No, they had already checked the steady advance of the allied armies, and they would do it again, for the Fatherland, for *Heimat*, for home.

Then the storm broke on the line of old trenches.
The shells rained down, down, down.
For forty minutes the shells arced over the trenches,
Drumming the ground with relentless intensity.
'Here they come' someone shouted.
Nervous hands gripped rifles, fumbled with grenades;
The *Sturmtruppen* would soon be upon them.

Percy was hit. Fearful explosions pulverised the line. There was nowhere to go, nowhere to run. All the Welsh boys could do was grind their faces into the soil and hope against hope that they would survive.

Then the Germans appeared, the silhouettes of their *Stahlhelme* – steel helmets – distinctive on the skyline. They were well equipped, their special machine guns fired from their hips as they walked over. They threw long-handled grenades that travelled far and exploded with a vicious bark.

Picking themselves out of the destruction, the boy soldiers of the 17th aimed their rifles and fired, although some, fearing the worst, and close to panic, forgot even how to load them, to work the bolt relentlessly in the heat of the action. Seizing the moment, a brave Welsh sergeant jumped from the trench and picked up a Lewis gun; he was

not going to let his lads be overrun. No, he would do what he could to stop the Germans.

Overhead, British shells were answering the call of an S.O.S. rocket fired from the trenches. They were bursting with vicious intent above the attackers, a deadly rain of steel shards and shrapnel bullets, and the German line was wavering. A gallant *Unteroffizier* – another sergeant – had made it to the Welsh line. He too had led his men – boys just like Percy – bravely in battle, and now he lay where he died, across the parapet, *Gefallen für das Vaterland*, fallen for the Fatherland.

'Raid repulsed,' read the 17th Battalion record, 'leaving one dead Hun in our lines. Casualties, 19'. The adjutant finished his matter-of-fact record, and turned to his letters.

In the fading light, he wrote the familiar phrase, 'I regret to inform you that your son was wounded in action'.

WOUNDED

'STRETCHER-BEARERS! STRETCHER-BEARERS!'

It was a cry that no soldier ever wanted to hear. Hurriedly, bearers of the 17th RWF, boys of the Red Dragon, worked their way through the wreckage to get those who had been wounded. They had to act quickly if the stricken boys were to stand any chance of survival.

And one of them was Percy, the boy-soldier from Cefn Mawr.

Percy was badly wounded in the back. A shell had burst close to him and one of its awful splinters had hurt him terribly.

The pit boy from Cefn lay still in the broken trench. Great waves of pain wracked his body. As he lost consciousness he cried out, 'Mam... Mam...', just as so many other mother's boys had done before him in the foreign fields of Flanders and Picardy.

Working quickly, the stretcher-bearers did their best to dress the wound, just as they had for his brother two years before. But now their job was to get Percy on his way to the aid post, and on to the hospital – as soon as was possible, if he was to stand a chance.

'Alright bach, alright', said the bearers, 'you'll be fine matey, you'll see'. It seemed that they'd said that soothing lie a thousand times before.

In this war, many soldiers hoped for a simple wound that would get them back home, to Blighty – wounds that could be treated simply in the comfort of an army hospital in Britain. But no soldier would have wished to have the wound that felled poor Percy in that dreadful trench raid.

He was taken to the Advanced Dressing Station in Lechelle. Here, gentle medics worked hard to clean his wound with carbolic acid – no doubt the same antiseptic made by the Graessers in Ruabon. They packed the gaping wound with gauze so that it was protected, and wrapped the wounded soldier in pure white bandages – so white that they were in stark contrast to the dirty body and grimy uniform of the boy from the trenches, of the pit boy from Wales. He was not alone; that day sixty-five other men lay waiting on stretchers; the war was still grinding out terrible statistics. The fighting would be over soon, they said; but the medics of that station ignored what they heard – they saw only a stream of terrible wounds in innocent bodies.

'Ok, send him down the line'

The Medical Officer barked out his order and moved on to the next man. He had work to do, and every boy was a mother's son.

The RAMC medical men picked up Percy's stretcher, already soaked in blood, and loaded him into the ambulance, which jolted sickeningly over the shelled and rutted roads as it motored back through the zone of devastation.

The medical men had seen many terrible sights over this war, and had suffered themselves as they looked at the broken humanity in their ambulances. These were memories that no man could forget. But for now, at least, they were immune to the suffering. They had a job to do. After all, Percy's wound was no different from the many others they

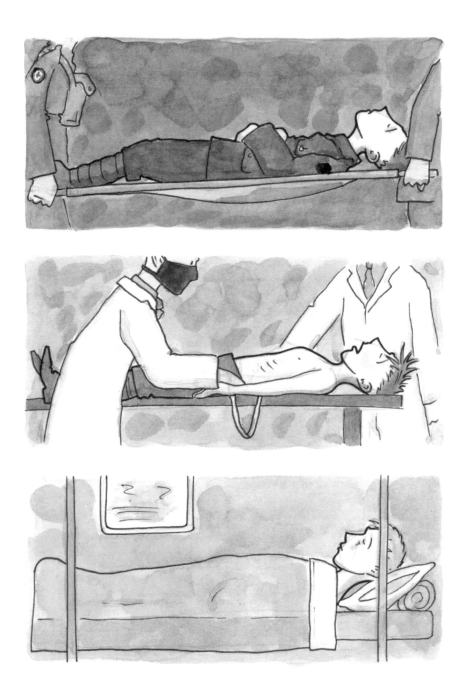

had treated; but with that loss of blood, time was critical. Adjusting goggles against the wind and pulling his collars up, the driver stuck to his task. And all the while Percy was barely conscious, jarred awake only by the pain that broke in waves across his body, made worse by the solid rocking of the motor.

Percy's destination was a hospital near the sea. Loaded onto a train at the Casualty Clearing Station, there were nurses to tend him; military women trained in the treatment of wounded soldiers, women who had seen the worst that men could do to each other, but carried on, regardless. Briskly efficient, the white-uniformed nurses tended to the often filthy, wounded men in their bunks, and saw them on their way. For those men, used only to the inhumanity of the trenches, the presence of the nurses calmed them.

As Percy lay there on the brink of consciousness, there was a voice that reminded him of his best girl, of his London girl born of a Welsh mother, of Kitty. And all the while her precious letters, her simple photo, and the watch that kept them together, travelled with him to his destination. They would stay with him, always.

The long, long, hospital train was bound for Boulogne. The Sea! At Boulogne the gulls dipped and dived as they had done at Llandudno; in those glorious days of summer when Percy walked with Kitty, and had ices on the pier. But here there was no time for trivialities, no memory of peace; for in the hospitals near the dunes at Wimereux there was space for twenty-thousand wounded men.

And one of those was Percy. He was just one of the many thousands, men who had passed through the medical chain from the grime and corruption of the trenches to reach their own peace. That peace was in the clean white sheets and the smell of carbolic; whispered voices and brisk steps. Percy did not have to hold a rifle any more, and though the pain was intense, he was content. He would see his girl again, his Kitty, his servant girl from Argoed Hall.

Perhaps they could plan for a time when they had their own brick cottage, Percy a coal hewer like his father, the king of the miners; Kitty cooking bakestones on her own griddle.

But suffering was all around him, and men cried out in pain, men who had been wounded in the great advance of the Allied armies, men who had done their bit to hasten the end of the war.

Suddenly, he had an urge to write.

'Nurse! Please…can you help…' Percy's voice was barely legible, a hoarse whisper straining to be heard above the groaning and cries from the boys in the ward.

A young face strained by the war appeared at his bedside.

'There now, don't fret' the nurse said soothingly. Passing Percy the stubby pencil he had carried at all times in this war, she turned away from the young boy in front of her. There was no time for tears. She owed it to the other boys wrecked by this hateful war.

Percy picked up the pencil and with effort, and on a scrap of paper, wrote a letter to Kitty, to his best girl, to his loved one across the valley of his dreams.

23 September 1918
Dear Kitty
Just a line hoping you are alright. I am in hospital and as you will see by the writing I am not in a very good position. I am waiting to come across to Blighty. Tell Jack that he was very lucky not to come across here. Well I will close with best love
Yours truly
Percy
Sealed with a loving kiss

The nurse folded the paper and passed it on to be posted, and dimmed the lights on the ward. Men cried out in the night, but Percy had written to his best girl, and sealed it with his kisses. He could rest now.

And his best girl would hold those kisses dear for the rest of her life.

The rest of her life.

28 September 1918
No 83 General Hospital
Boulogne Base
British Expeditionary Force

Dear Mrs Edwards
As I very much feared yesterday, I have today to send along the sad news which you have doubtless already received, that your boy passed peacefully away here at 4.30 this afternoon. I saw him a few times today, but he was too far gone to recognise me; and thus he passed gradually away to the better world where there will be no more wars and weeping.

May the God of all comfort and consolation be your strength and stay during these hours of sorrow. Your sorrow may be a proud sorrow, for your son has laid down his life in a noble cause. Your faith can be a firm faith, for we do not pass on those without hope. It is only 'Good night,' and soon the day must dawn and the shadows end. We can look forward – when we shall receive gladness and joy, and sorrow and sighing shall flee away.

Your boy was a good Christian witness, he was true to the good principles in which he has been brought up, and we all miss him. With my prayers in sympathy,
Yours sincerely
Percival M. Despres (Chaplain)

THE GREAT WAR ENDED AT 11 AM ON 11 NOVEMBER 1918.
THE BOYS OF THE RED DRAGON HAD PLAYED THEIR PART.

ONE OF THEM, PERCY EDWARDS FROM CEFN MAWR,
WAS LAID TO REST IN THE GREAT CEMETERY OF TERLINCTHUN,
GRAVES BY THE SEA.

AND IT WAS HERE THE KING CAME WHEN THE GUNS FELL SILENT;
TRAVELLING SIMPLY AS A PILGRIM, WITH NO TRAPPINGS OF STATE,
OR POMP, OR CEREMONY.

IT WAS HERE THAT THE KING CAME;
CAME TO SEE PERCY.

AND TO REMEMBER.
AND TO NEVER FORGET.

———————

PERCY'S STORY

Percy is a true story, based on the life of one young soldier plucked from his pit village in North Wales in 1918. In many ways, Percy's story is typical of the many thousands of young men of eighteen who were sent to fight in the last year of the war, and who would make up a significant part of the armies that fought in France in 1918.

Percy's story is based on a parcel of letters, letters that had been kept by Kitty, his sweetheart. By chance, these letters survived intact. They provide the framework to a remarkable story, a story spelling out a life of a young man of Wales before and after he joined the army. The letters describe his hopes and fears, the basics of his training, and his brief time at the front. Through them we learn of the life of a typical young man from rural Wales who was to serve his country in war.

But developing his story further required access to a remarkable set of documents, sources and other material to give breadth to his tale. Some of these are given below, presented chapter by chapter, so that readers may explore Percy's story further for themselves, and perhaps be inspired to follow stories of their own.

Pit Boy

Slightly built he was bulked out in rough tweed.... This picture of Percy is drawn from the image of William Davenport, a pit boy and survivor of the Pretoria Mine disaster, Lancashire, of 21 December 1910. Davenport was only one of two to escape the mine explosion which claimed the lives of 344 men. Alan Davies, *The Pretoria Pit Disaster* (Amberley, Stroud, 2013)

Beneath the rough stone cap... Details of Cefn Mawr, its history, and its industries can be found in the document *Cefn Mawr and District: Understanding Urban Character* (Cadw, Cardiff, 2014)

Percy had been a pit boy from the age of fourteen... The *Coal Mines Act, 1911 (Part IV)* stated that 'No boy under the age of fourteen years... shall be employed in or allowed to be for the purpose of employment in any mine below ground.'

Working for eight-hour shifts... The *Coal Mines Regulation Act, 1908* was introduced by the Liberal Government in 1908 in order to restrict the length of time a miner could spend below ground – limited to eight hours. David Lloyd-George was one of its main architects.

In 1918, at fifty-three years of age... details of Benjamin Edwards' family is taken from the 1911 Census returns, available at The National Archives in Kew, London, or various sources online.

Cymru

As the war came in 1914 there were over two-hundred-and-thirty thousand men... details from Ivor Nicholson & Trevor Lloyd-Williams, *Wales: Its Part in the War*, (Hodder & Stoughton, London, 1919), p. 74; Robin Barlow, *Wales and World War One* (Gomer, Ceredigion, 2014), p.178

*Cefn lad killed in Astley Pit... Cefn Chronicle,*1916

Food of the engines... Wales: Its Part in the War, p. 71; *Wales and World War One,* p. 179.

Long dreary rows of drab houses... Wales: Its Part in the War, p. 73; p. 141 onwards also describes the condition of housing in South Wales.

North Wales coal...' Wales: Its Part in the War, p. 114; *The North Wales Coalfield,* (National Coal Board, 1953)

Keep the Home Fires Burning... Originally called 'Till the Boys Come Home', this patriotic song was written by Welshman David Ivor Davies (Ivor Novello) and Lena Guilbert Ford in October 1914, becoming popular in 1915.

For King and Country

Wales must do her duty... Lloyd-George's speech at the Queen's Hall, London, 19 September 1914, published as David Lloyd-George, *The Great War, Speech* (Hodder & Stoughton, London, 1914), p.15.

Your King & Country Need You... A version of this appeared in local and national newspapers from 5 August onwards. For example, in the *Liverpool Evening Express*, it appeared almost every day for two weeks.

Too many good men lay in the Transvaal... Some 22,000 men of the British Army died in the Boer War of 1899-1902, most of them from disease.

Royal Welsh Fusiliers... The RWF was one of the most significant regiments to fight in the Great War, and raised a large number of battalions. See Captain J.C. Dunn, *The War the Infantry Knew 1914-1919.* (Abacus, London, 1994). In author Robert Graves' view 'The Royal Welch record was beyond reproach', *Goodbye to All That* (Jonathan Cape, London, 1929), p. 117; Graves served with the 2nd Battalion RWF.

Blue enlistment papers... Each recruit filled out a 'Certified Copy of Attestation', Army Form B2512A, which gave all his details, and which recorded the oath he had taken to King & Country. On filling in the form and being accepted, he received a shilling coin, his first day's wage as a soldier, known as the 'King's Shilling'.

The Great War

Many soldier's memoirs give details of life at the front. One of the best was written by Capt. F.C. Hitchcock '*Stand To' A Diary of the Trenches 1915-1918* (Hurst & Blackett, London, 1937), and there is much in Capt. J.C. Dunn, *The War the Infantry Knew 1914-1919.* (Abacus, London, 1994).

Two lines of ditches could be seen… Trench warfare changed and evolved throughout the war, from simple ditches to complex trenches. The life of the soldier in the trenches is described by Peter Doyle & Chris Foster, *Remembering Tommy, The British Soldier of the Great War* (History Press, Stroud, 2013).

Letters home were sparse… British soldiers' letters and cards were censored by their own officers, and tended to have few details. German letters tend to have more information at the time. See Peter Doyle & Rob Schäfer, *Fritz & Tommy, Across the Barbed Wire* (History Press, Stroud, 2015) for details.

In the pink… This phrase was often used by soldiers, when there was nothing else they could write. See Peter Doyle & Julian Walker, *Trench Talk* (History Press, Stroud, 2012)

Corporal Lowell… Cefn Chronicle, 29 July 1916

Lance Corporal Hughes… Cefn Chronicle, 27 May 1916

Mr Richards' General Store…. Adverts for E. Richards, 'Grocer and Provision Dealer' from the Gwalia Stores in Cefn were a regular feature of the *Cefn Chronicle.*

Servant Girl

Robert Graesser came from Saxony... Robert Graesser's chemical works is described in *Cefn Mawr and District: Understanding Urban Character* (Cadw, Cardiff, 2014, p.21, 80)

Argoed Hall was a grand house... Argoed Hall is a listed building, now a private residential building. See http://orapweb.rcahms.gov.uk/coflein//C/CPG063.pdf. The 1901 and 1911 Census returns reveals the family and servants at the hall – though before Kitty's time there.

Kitty's was just sixteen... Details from the census, 1911, 182 King's Road, Chelsea

'General Domestic' servants... See the article Matthew Woollard, *The Classification of Domestic Servants in England and Wales 1851-1951* (Proceedings of the Servant Project, Oslo, 2002) http://privatewww.essex.ac.uk/~matthew/Papers/Woollard_ClassificationofDomesticServants.pdf

Kitty's mother was a native Welsh speaker... Details from the 1911 census.

The language of stamps... The placement of stamps at odd angles on envelopes and postcards was used in the early twentieth century so send messages, usually a hidden language of love.

Immense bridge of nineteen spans... The aqueduct is a UNESCO World Hertiage Site, see https://www.pontcysyllte-aqueduct.co.uk

Nineteen-Eighteen

Mametz Wood... Is forever associated with the actions of the 38th (Welsh) Division. A good description of the action is given by Robin Barlow, *Wales and World War One* (Gomer, Ceredigion, 2014), p.59–85.

Robbie Jones of Acrefair... Cefn Chronicle 26 August 1916. In fact, Robbie Jones had returned from the USA to his aunt in Acrefair to join the army.

Corporal Hughes of Rock Terrace... Cefn Chronicle 26 August 1916

Battle of the Somme shown at The George Edwards Hall... The screening of the film 'The Battle of the Somme' at the George Edwards Hall in early November 1916 was advertised in *Cefn Chronicle,* which described it as 'A battlefield in reality - magnificent and terrible'

Chronicl y Cefn carried cheery adverts... The whole front page of the *Cefn Chronicle* was given over to such adverts, for Williams & Watkin, J.E. Jones the pharmacist, and C. Jones the draper.

Backs against the wall... see Gary Sheffield, *The Chief: Douglas Haig and the British Army* (Aurum, London, 2012)

He flung the full weight of a great army... *Cefn Chronicle* April 1918

Thousands of battle-hardened Frontkämpfer... David Jones, who served with the 15th Royal Welsh Fusiliers, uses this term in a dedication in his book *In Parenthesis* (Faber & Faber, London, 1963, p. 'to the enemy Front-Fighters who shared our pains...'

Gone for a Soldier

Services Rendered... Every serviceman and woman who was discharged from the army due to illness or wounding was awarded a 'Silver War Badge', each one with a special number to ensure it was not misused.

The War Office had a solution... The introduction of conscription in the *Military Service Act, 1916* meant that *'Every male British subject who... had attained the age of eighteen years...shall be deemed to have been duly enlisted in His Majesty's regular services'.*

I'r fyddin fechgyn Gwalia!... Welsh-language recruiting poster printed in December 1914 https://www.iwm.org.uk/collections/item/object/27867

Taller (or cockier) boys would talk... See Richard Van Emden, *Boy Soldiers of the Great War* (Headline, London, 2006)

Almost half a million more men... See *Statistics of the Military Effort of the British Empire during the Great War 1914-1920* (HMSO, London, 1922).

Percy received his papers... Percy's military service record exists; most were destroyed in an air raid during the Second World War. There was a one in five chance that his record would survive.

Mr Edwards chipped in... the matchbox was listed in Army Form 104-126, the list of Percy's objects returned to the family, in 1919, part of Percy's surviving Service record.

Percy's mam had seen David's feet... 'Trench foot' was a serious affliction caused by prolonged immersion of the feet in water, which prevented blood flow and led to gangrene.

Taking out his pocket-knife... a series of soldiers' graffiti messages was discovered in a railway tunnel near Llangollen in 2007 http://news.bbc.co.uk/1/hi/wales/north_east/6269586.stm

Sniggery Camp

'The first night we got here...' Letter to Kitty, 22 June 1918

The Cefn lad had been called to Sniggery Camp... Pte Percy Edwards, Service record

Percy the recruit stood just five feet... Pte Percy Edwards, Service record, Medical History Sheet

Sniggery Camp was home to the 3rd Battalion... Details from The Royal Welsh museum, http://royalwelsh.org.uk/downloads/B07-09-SWB-WW1-3rdTrgGradYSBattalions.pdf

Arrival at the camp was always a challenge... The experience of young recruits in camp in 1918 is described in the account by Frederick James Hodges, *Men of 18 in 1918* (Arthur Stockwell, London, 1988)

Nearby, bordering the low fields... Contemporary pictures show recruits training on the beach; today Sir Antony Gormley's figures from the installation *Another Place*, look out to sea, just as recruits once did in 1918.

'I'm writing these few lines...' Letter to Kitty, 13 August 1918

'Well, I've settled down...' Letter to Kitty, July 1918

'I'm glad to hear to have a grand...', meaning a 'grand time', Letter to Kitty, 6 June 1918

'We went to a place called Seaforth...' Letter to Kitty, 6 June 1918

In Training

Pattern 1908 Infantry Equipment... Instructions published by the War Office in 1908, *The Pattern 1908 Web Infantry Equipment*, see http://www.karkeeweb.com/patterns/1908/manuals/08_FI_May_1908_R1.pdf

To build Percy up... The soldiers' training programme had been set out in in the early part of the Twentieth Century; see War Office, *Infantry Training (4-Company Organisation)*, HMSO, London, 1914).

We have all been vaccinated... Letter to Kitty, July 1918

I have stuck it so far... Letter to Kitty, July 1918

And as the new fresh-faced... described in the account by Frederick James Hodges, *Men of 18 in 1918* (Arthur Stockwell, London, 1988). In July 1918, Percy wrote to Kitty, 'My face is properly sun burnt'.

A man came round our huts... Letter to Kitty, July 1918

You should have seen us today... Letter to Kitty, July 1918

Just as that song says, pack all your troubles... Letter to Kitty, July 1918. *Pack Up Your Troubles in Your Old Kit Bag* was a hit song written in 1915 by two brothers from St Asaph, North Wales – George and Felix Powell.

To France

Jack was at Kinmel... Kinmel was a large military camp in North Wales http://www.coflein.gov.uk/en/site/401319/details/kinmel-military-camp-bodelwyddan

I am trying to get a transfer to the RWF... Letter to Kitty, July 1918

I've got two brothers in the Royal Welsh... Letter to Kitty, July 1918

But it was not to be... Pte Percy Edwards, Service Record; he went to France as a soldier of the South Wales Borderers.

Six Victoria Crosses... Soldiers of the RWF had won the VC six times between April 1915 and October 1917; two more would be awarded in August and September 1918. See R.A. Skaife, *A Short History of the Royal Welch Fusiliers* (Gale & Polden, Aldershot, 1940).

I think it will be a long while... Letter to Kitty, 20 August 1918

I had a very pleasant journey... Letter to Kitty, 20 August 1918

At the Base

The life of the soldier in France is described by Peter Doyle & Chris Foster, *Remembering Tommy, The British Soldier of the Great War* (History Press, Stroud, 2013).

Don-nay mwa ah man-jay, sil-voo-play... There were many phrasebooks produced for soldiers' use, this was taken from *The British Soldier's Anglo-French Pocket Dictionary*, a contemporary soldier's phrasebook.

He took one of the peculiar postcards... Field Service Post Card, 16 August 1918. Pre-prepared, these cards were sent in times of difficulty to keep families informed of what was happening to their loved ones.

Just a brief note to let you know I'm in the Pink... Letter to Kitty, 20 August 1918

Some of my pals are going home... Letter to Kitty, 13 August 1918

The land that soldiers called Blighty... This soldiers' slang term for Britain was derived from the Hindustani word for home, and was adopted by the British Army in India, see Peter Doyle & Julian Walker, *Trench Talk* (History Press, Stroud, 2012).

The 38th, some 16,000 men of Lloyd George's army... The 38th (Welsh) Division was raised in the aftermath of Lloyd George's great speech on 29 September 1914. Some background is given in Lt-Col. J.E. Munby *A History of the 38th (Welsh) Division* (Hugh Rees, London, 1920) and Anon, *Welsh Army Corps, Report of the Executive Committee* (Western Mail, Cardiff, 1921)

Hommes 40, Chevaux 8... This was the experience of most soldiers moving up the line, who were surprised to see they were herded into bare trucks that could serve *either* men, *or* horses

H! Monsieur? Water. Eau?... The troop trains often moved incredibly slowly, due to the amount rail traffic needed to serve the army in Northern France. Soldiers in their bare trucks often hopped out and ran to the engine to get hot water for tea.

Up the Line

I have been transferred to the RWF... Letter to Kitty, 10 September 1918

The 17th Battalion 'The 17th RWF ...was originally formed on the 2nd February [1915]...The headquarters of the Battalion was at Charlton Street, Llandudno' Lt-Col. J.E. Munby *A History of the 38th (Welsh) Division* (Hugh Rees, London, 1920), p. 4.

In August 1918, the boys of the 17th... War Diary, 17th Battalion RWF, 'August 25th, Battalion rested 2 hours in the trenches, – at 3 a.m. marched by compass bearing to 1000 yds N.W. of Mametz Wood...'

The Stretcher bearers had picked up David Edwards... Record from the 'Roll of Individuals entitled to the "War Badge"', badge number 105217, shows that Dai Edwards enlisted on 31 December 1914, and had been invalided out of the army, due to wounds received in attack at Mametz, by 18 September 1916.

'Fine night and morning'... Douglas Haig: War Diaries and Letters 1914-1918 (edited by Gary Sheffield and John Bourne, Weidenfeld & Nicholson, London, 2005), Diary entry for 8 August, p. 439.

'Dear Kitty' he wrote... Letter to Kitty, 10 September 1918.

The Trenches

The Edwards family picked out a letter... Cefn Chronicle, 1916

The 38th Division pushed towards the Siegfried Stellung... 'On 11 September [they]...were brought up against the celebrated Hindenberg Line' Lt-Col. J.E. Munby *A History of the 38th (Welsh) Division* (Hugh Rees, London, 1920), p. 62. The Germans called their lines the *Siegfried Stellung*, the British, the Hindenburg Line.

The old trenches of 1916 were once more held... 'The frontline was taken over by the 115th Brigade and occupied what had been the support trench of a system...' Lt-Col. J.E. Munby *A History of the 38th (Welsh) Division* (Hugh Rees, London, 1920), p. 62. The 17th RWF formed part of the 115th Brigade.

I have had no time to write... Letter to Kitty, 10 September 1918

The shock of the exploding shells... The sounds of bursting shells have been recorded by many men who served at the front; Robert Graves, of the 2nd RWF described his first experience in his book *Goodbye to All That* (Jonathan Cape, London, 1929), p. 131: 'A German shell came over and then whoo-oo-oooooOOO – bump – CRASH!'.

Fritz caught a few of our chaps... Letter to Kitty, 10 September 1918. 'Fritz' was a common nickname for German soldiers in this part of the war. The 17th Battalion RWF war diary gives details of the attack.

17th RWF to push out patrols... War Diary, 17th Battalion RWF, 12
  September 1918

His beloved wristwatch glowed... listed in Army Form 104-126, the list of
  Percy's objects returned to the family in 1919.

HALT!... The standard challenge of a sentry. Returning trench-raiders were
  often in danger from their own men.

Trench Raid

'Lechelle, 13 September 1918...' War Diary, 17th Battalion RWF, 13
  September 1918

Lieutenant-Colonel Beasley... was the commanding officer of the 17th
  Battalion RWF.

Army Form C.2118... was the standard printed form produced for army
  units to record their war diaries on; war diaries had to be kept while a
  unit was 'in the field'.

Then the Germans appeared... the attack was described by Captain J.C. Dunn
  in *The War the Infantry Knew 1914-1919*. (Abacus, London, 1994),
  pp. 539–540: 'September 13th... The Germans were coming over the
  skyline in extended order ... Two men were carrying a light machine
  gun, one firing the gun from the hip'

A brave Welsh sergeant jumped... *The War the Infantry Knew 1914-1919*, p.
  540: '...Sergeant Lee picked up a Lewis gun, jumped out on top, and,
  getting a position for the gun, shot eight of [the attackers]...'

Overhead, British shells were answering the call of an SOS rocket... *The War the
  Infantry Knew 1914–1919*, p. 539: '...Someone fired the rifle holding
  the SOS rocket...'

A gallant unteroffizier... *The War the Infantry Knew 1914-1919*, p. 541: 'A
  German NCO was lying almost on the parapet. When his section began

to fall back he ran forward alone, and threw a bomb... with another bomb in his raised hand when someone shot him. It was a stout effort'

Raid repulsed... War Diary, 17th Battalion RWF, 13 September 1918, 9.50 am. The war Diary records that this raid resulted in nineteen Royal Welsh casualties.

'I regret to inform you...' This was the typical form of words used in letters written to inform relatives of death or wounding. The Edwards family received two telegrams after Percy had been wounded, the first 'Regret to inform you that your son 93606 Pte Percy Edwards, Royal Welch Fusiliers, dangerously ill, 25th September at 83 General Hospital, Boulogne, France. Regret permission to visit cannot be granted.' Three days later, another telegram reported his death 'Deeply regret to inform you your son...died from wounds 28 September'.

Wounded

The wounding, evacuation and treatment of soldiers during the Great War has been described by Emily Mayhew, *Wounded, From Battlefield to Blighty 1914-1918.* (The Bodley Head, London, 2013)

Stretcher-bearers!... Stretcher-bearers were battalion men, infantrymen who carried no weapons in battle, but who went over in battle to recover the wounded.

Percy was badly wounded in the back... Pte Percy Edwards, Military Record.

'Mam, mam...' Soldiers under distress often called for their mother; See Lieut Wyn Griffith, *Up To Mametz* (Faber & Faber, London, 1931), p.235: '...after a thunderous crash in our ears [the young soldier] began to cry out for his mother, in a thin boyish voice, 'Mam, mam...'. Wyn Griffith served with the 15th RWF.

In this war, many soldiers hoped for a simple wound... 'Blighty' wounds, those which were not life threatening, were often hoped for as they allowed soldiers to get home, invalided out of the army, described by Pte Frank Richards, *Old Soldiers Never Die* (The author, no date). Richards served in the 2nd RWF.

He was taken to the Advanced Dressing Station in Lechelle... 13 September 1918, 131 Field Ambulance RAMC [38th Division] Adm GSW shell back.

He was not alone that day... 131 Field Ambulance War Diary, 'LECHELLE 13-9-18, Admitted 8 sick, 65 wounded. Evacuated 58 remaining 5'

'Ok, send him down the line'... The casualty chain went from an aid station in the trench, to the Advanced Dressing Stations, run by Royal Army Medical Corps (RAMC) soldiers of a unit known as the Field Ambulance, then moving to a Casualty Clearing Station, which might hold 1000 casualties at any one time, before being sent to a base hospital by train. See http://www.longlongtrail.co.uk/soldiers/a-soldiers-life-1914-1918/the-evacuation-chain-for-wounded-and-sick-soldiers/

Percy's destination was by the sea... A letter returned to Kitty had been addressed to Percy in No 83, General Hospital, Boulogne, France

For in the hospitals at Wimereux there was space... There were numerous hospitals in this area close to Boulogne, twenty in total, capable of caring for some 20,000 casualties http://www.remembrancetrails-northernfrance.com/history/the-rearguard/the-british-military-presence-on-the-coast-of-northern-france.html

Percy picked up his pencil... Percy's last letter home to Kitty, sent on 23 September 1918; Percy died just five days later.

Dear Mrs Edwards... Letter published in the *Cefn Chronicle*, November 1918. The hospital Chaplain, Percival Despres, wrote to Percy's parents, and this letter was reproduced in the Chronicle. The Rev. Percival Montburn Despres, R.A.Ch.D had previously served as a RAMC private and was used to the suffering of soldiers. Percy's death was also announced in the *North Wales Guardian* Friday November 8th, 1918: 'Mr and Mrs Benjamin Edwards, Rock Place, have received the sad news that their son, Pte Percy Edwards, R.W.F., who joined the army in April and only went to France in August, has died of wounds in the No. 83 General Hospital, Boulogne, France. He was only 18 years old in February and much regret is expressed at his early death.'

One of them, Percy... see the Commonwealth War Graves Commission record https://www.cwgc.org/find-war-dead/casualty/4025228/edwards,-/

It was here the King came... King George V visited Terlincthun Cemetery, the last of his pilgrimage, where he made a speech: '...Standing beneath this Cross of Sacrifice, facing the great Stone of Remembrance, and encompassed by these sternly simple headstones, we remember, and must charge our children to remember, that, as our dead were equal in sacrifice, so they are equal in honour...' *The King's Pilgrimage,* (Hodder & Stoughton, London, 1922). One of those 'sternly simple headstones' was Percy's.

ACKNOWLEDGEMENTS

WRITING *Percy* HAS BEEN A LONG AND REWARDING journey supported by the belief of others. It is a remarkable story that could not have been told without the help and assistance of many people. The letters came to me with the hope that I would do something with them; this has been my mission. Jo De Vries and Emma Parkin have been unstinting in their belief, incredible ambassadors for the project, tirelessly working with the text to improve it, and to guide me. Tim Godden's amazing illustrations, born out of expert knowledge for the subject, were always seen as a foundation for the story, and I thank him for working with me on it. Claire Lewis gave her time, local knowledge and support to the project, and I am grateful for her help and enthusiasm. Nadia Imtiaz and a clutch of youthful readers kindly read the text for me. The insight and assistance of Ryan Gearing at Uniform has been essential to the project. I am grateful for the advice and support of my friends Chris Foster, Julian Walker and Robin Schäfer. I thank Michael Morpurgo for taking the time to read the text amongst his other commitments, and for providing his own words. I could not have completed this book without the love of Julie and

James, who are always my foundation. Finally, Libby Simpson has been an inspiration, so insightful, and so invested in the life of Percy – living his every moment – in many ways, his story so similar to that of her uncle, Albert Howard, a young man who also died of wounds in France, aged eighteen, in 1918. This story equally is his, and that of every other lad of eighteen who faced dangers I could never imagine.